First Day to Final Grade

Second Edition

A Graduate Student's Guide to Teaching

Anne Curzan and Lisa Damour

Ann Arbor

The University of Michigan Press

Copyright © by the University of Michigan 2000, 2006
All rights reserved
Published in the United States of America by
The University of Michigan Press
Manufactured in the United States of America
⊗ Printed on acid-free paper

2009   2008   2007   2006   4   3   2   1

A CIP catalog record for this book is available from the British Library.

U.S. CIP data applied for.

ISBN-13: 978-0-472-03188-7
ISBN-10: 0-472-03188-0

First Day to Final Grade

Contents

Introduction   1

Chapter 1. Becoming a Teacher   5
    Your Teaching Persona   5
    The Joys of Teaching   6
    The Agonies of Teaching   7
    Maintaining Perspective   9

Chapter 2. The First Day of the Term   11
    Before Classes Begin   11
    Outfitting Yourself   13
    Introducing Yourself   15
    Establishing Contact   20
    Syllabus: Setting the Agenda   22
    The First Class Meeting   24

Chapter 3. Weekly Class Preparation   31
    The Goal of the Class   31
    The Lesson Plan   33
    Time Management   38
    Organizing Space   39
    Interacting with the Professor   41
    Addressing Problems   43

Chapter 4. Running a Discussion   45
    Discussions versus Task-Based Participation   45
    Arranging the Classroom   46
    Initiating Student Participation   46
    Effective Discussion Questions   50
    Facilitating Discussion   53

Handling Sensitive Material   56
Handling Discussion-Stopping Students   57
Wrapping up Discussion   62

Chapter 5. Problem Sets and Laboratories   65
Teaching with Problem Sets   65
Ways to Review Problem Sets   67
Eliciting Student Feedback   73
Grading Problem Sets   74
Running an Experimental Lab   75
Common Problems in Labs   79
Lab Reports   80

Chapter 6. Trusty Class Plans   83
Information Exchange   83
Debate   85
Pros and Cons   89
Consolidating Lists   91
Video Presentation   92
Guest Speaker   93
Exam Preparation   96
Grammar and Usage Review   99
Paper Workshop   101

Chapter 7. One-on-One Interaction with Students   106
Office Hours   106
E-mail   109
Students with Attendance Problems   111
Students with Learning Disabilities   112
Students with Personal Problems   114
Antagonistic Students   117
Fraternizing with Students   120
Sexual Harassment   122
Plagiarism   125
Cheating   131
Grade Complaints   132
Letters of Recommendation   138

Chapter 8. Grading   141
>   Grade Calculations   141
>   Grade Books   141
>   Grading Exams   143
>   Grading Papers   145
>   Grading Problem Sets   154
>   Grading Lab Reports   155
>   Grading Group Work   156
>   Handing Back Graded Material   158
>   In-Class Review of Exams   160
>   Late Work   162
>   Missed Exams   162
>   Calculating Final Grades   163

Chapter 9. Feedback from Students   166
>   General Informal Feedback from Students   166
>   Specific Informal Feedback from Students   167
>   Formal Feedback from Students   169

Chapter 10. The Balance of School and Teaching   175
>   Front-Loading Effort   175
>   Assigning Responsibility   175
>   Scheduling Teaching-Related Activities   177
>   Coordinating Teaching and Personal Schedules   179
>   Self-Preservation   180

Appendixes   183
>   Appendix A. Sample Course Syllabus   185
>   Appendix B. Lesson Plan for a Discussion Class   187
>   Appendix C. Lesson Plan for a Lecture Class   189
>   Appendix D. Annotated Text with Questions   190
>   Appendix E. Guidelines for a Paper Workshop   192
>   Appendix F. Guidelines for Writing a Peer Response   195
>   Appendix G. Sample Letters of Recommendation   197
>   Appendix H. Midterm Feedback Form   200

Index   201

Introduction

This book is designed to be an accessible, pragmatic teaching guide on a wide range of issues that arise both inside and outside the classroom for many first-time teaching assistants. The advice stems not only from our own experiences in the classroom but also from extensive consultation with other experienced teaching assistants as well as university faculty in a variety of disciplines who are highly regarded for their teaching skills. Important principles in pedagogical theory underlie much of the material presented here, and all our advice is grounded in broader pedagogical approaches. But our focus remains on the practical, day-to-day matters you will face as a teaching assistant and how you can approach them effectively.

Graduate students teaching in university settings face unique issues in the classroom. Much of the material in this book will be helpful to new teachers at other stages in their careers, but some of the material is aimed directly at new graduate student teachers.

We strongly recommend that you familiarize yourself with the excellent material published on pedagogy in higher education, and we offer suggested readings throughout this book. We also recognize that not all theoretical material on pedagogy aims to provide practical advice (on such banal matters as when to do your photocopying); we offer this book as a complementary resource for first-time teaching assistants. There is great value to theoretical material about teaching; there is also great value to practical advice.

The kind of collaboration that has created this book is one of the keys to successful teaching at every level. We all develop as teachers throughout our careers as we learn from our own experiences as well as the experiences of others. Much of this collaboration happens informally—over lunch or during a chance meeting in the hallway. Some of it happens more formally during pedagogical workshops or training sessions. In this book, we have tried to record a range of teaching wisdom so that first-time teachers will have immediate access to a teaching resource when there is no workshop planned and the hallways are empty.

Organization of the Book

Each topic in this book is divided into headings and subheadings for easy reference. You will find a detailed table of contents in the front to help you locate exactly what you need at any given point (or moment of crisis) during the term.

Each chapter includes explanations and examples, from handouts to conversations. There are appendixes at the end of the book with longer exemplary documents. In each chapter, we also share "teaching anecdotes" that we have collected, just so you know that whatever happens to you (especially if it is embarrassing or painful), someone else has probably experienced something similar, if not worse! At the end of each chapter you will find a short list of possible further readings should you wish to pursue a particular topic; we have limited these references to generally relevant books, many of which contain excellent bibliographies with more specifically directed books and articles.

Terminology

Teaching Assistant

Graduate students at different universities prefer different terms for referring to their teaching role in the classroom: teaching assistant, graduate student instructor, graduate instructor, and so on. We had to pick one, and we settled on *teaching assistant*. There are connotation problems with *teaching assistant,* the most important of which is that it implies that the graduate student is necessarily helping a professor to teach, which is not always the case. Many graduate students run their own courses, and even those who run a section for a larger lecture course are still teaching on their own. The term *teaching assistant* is, however, the most widely accepted and used term for graduate students who teach; we hope no one will take offense at the selection of this term.

Singular Generic *They*

In writing general material about teaching assistants and students, it is impossible to avoid the "generic pronoun problem." Luckily, Anne has devoted (frighteningly) many research hours to this subject and, for better or worse, has strong views on the matter. Lisa, a psychologist, deferred to Anne, the linguist, entirely on this matter. Please send all contrary responses on this subject straight to Anne.

English does have a generic singular pronoun: it is *they*, and we almost all use it in the spoken language all the time. Grammar books finally have accepted that "generic *he*" is not generic, which leaves us with the "acceptable" option of *he or she*, but that can sound awkward (and it would make this book longer!). Grammarians state that while using *they* with a singular subject might create gender agreement, it violates number agreement. Not necessarily so. The pronoun *they* has taken on a singular function with singular subjects of unknown gender, and English speakers and readers are rarely significantly confused about the number of people in question (this change is not without precedence: *you*, formerly only plural, took on a singular function). We have opted, therefore, to be on the cutting edge of written language change, to stick to our guns, and to use singular *they*.

The Authors

Lisa Damour received a B.A. in psychology from Yale in 1992 and a Ph.D. in clinical psychology from the University of Michigan in May 1997. With all her newfound free time (if we ignore that she then started a postdoctoral fellowship), she decided to write a book with her friend and squash/swimming/running partner, Anne. Lisa worked as a teaching assistant for six semesters at the University of Michigan. She now has a private practice in Cleveland and is an adjunct faculty member at John Carroll University.

Anne Curzan received a B.A. in linguistics from Yale in 1991 and a Ph.D. in English from the University of Michigan in June 1998. To "complement" the work of writing her dissertation, she decided to write a book with her friend and squash/swimming/running partner, Lisa. Anne taught English for two years at a university in central China after graduating from college; she worked as a teaching assistant for six semesters at the University of Michigan and received the David and Linda Moscow Award for Excellence in the Teaching of Composition. She is now Associate Professor of English at the University of Michigan.

Since 2003, Lisa and Anne have been invited by the organizers of T.A. training programs around the country to present workshops or organize full programs for graduate student instructors.

Changes to the Second Edition

This new edition of *First Day to Final Grade* incorporates much of what we have learned about college teaching since we wrote the first edition of this book six years ago. Among other things, we have expanded our thinking on moving from class goals to class content, preparing for and running discussions, addressing problems within the class and with particular students, and responding to academic misconduct. The role of technology both inside and outside the classroom has changed significantly in the past six years, and we have updated our book to reflect these developments. We have also included new sample materials throughout the text and the appendixes.

Many of the changes that we've made for this new edition have grown out of our direct work with graduate student instructors at our home schools or at the universities where we have conducted T.A. training workshops or programs. We welcome the chance to grapple with the range and variety of challenges that face graduate student instructors and feel grateful for their willingness to share their experiences with us.

Acknowledgments

This book would not have been possible without the help and support of so many of our friends, colleagues, and mentors. In particular we would like to thank Matt Baker, Mary and Mike Curzan, Kate Gjaja, Karen Glennemeier, Johns Hopkins, Emily Hoyer, Darren Keefe, the late Glen Knudsvig, Rosemary Kowalski, Nathan Kutz, Sumati Murli, Chris Peterson, and Terri Tinkle for their time, meticulous reading, and invaluable comments on earlier versions of the manuscript. Special thanks also go to Doug Burger, Susan Montgomery, Fran Smith, and John Whittier-Ferguson, who all provided experienced advice on a multitude of teaching issues; to our students and instructors, who have taught us what it means to teach; and to Joel Smith, who provided, from the beginning, the backing that allowed our idea to become a book. Our families have given us unflagging support, counsel, and love throughout the process, and our friends have provided us with a never-ending supply of ideas and memorable quotes about teaching. For all of this and more, we are immeasurably grateful.

Chapter 1
Becoming a Teacher

Welcome to being a graduate student teaching assistant! Your mission is to enhance the education of undergraduate students. This is a challenging and exciting task which is often tinged with anxiety for first-time teachers.

While most graduate students are both eager to teach and nervous about teaching, universities have been slow to provide adequate training programs for first-time teachers. Stepping into the breach, we have written this book so you do not feel that you are starting from scratch. You will learn from your own experiences in the classroom, but we hope that the information in this book will spare you from repeating mistakes that others have already made.

> "The only advice I got before I started teaching was to erase the board using vertical strokes: erasing the board from side to side makes your butt wiggle."

Your department may or may not view your teaching responsibilities as a priority compared to your research and course work. But you should take this job seriously: you have been entrusted with the education of undergraduate students, which is a critical contribution to your department and to your field as a whole.

This chapter will supply some general advice about finding yourself in a classroom.

Your Teaching Persona

Teaching is a kind of performance, and the person you are in front of a classroom is in some ways different from the person you are the rest of the time. Developing your "teaching persona"—the person you become once you step into the classroom—takes time and experience.

Finding Your Teaching Persona

Over time, you will discover whether you, as an instructor, are loud or quiet, funny or serious, a sitter or a stander, a board user or a handout maven. In the meantime, experiment with different approaches until you figure out what feels comfortable and what elicits the best reaction from your students. Don't hesitate to try something that may not "feel like you," because your teaching persona may turn out to be an unexpected side of you. But do not be afraid to reject suggestions on teaching that you feel your innate personality will prevent you from pulling off (e.g., singing mnemonic devices). You will look uncomfortable and be less effective.

Teaching with Authority

For beginning teachers, there is often a progression from acting like you are in charge of the classroom to feeling like you are in charge of the classroom. This is normal. Unless you give them reason not to, students will generally accept your authority no matter how you feel about your qualifications as a teacher.

You will start to *feel* like you are in charge of your classroom as you gain experience. Until then, you may find that you rely more on "the rules" (guidelines, due dates, syllabi) and on established teacher-student roles to create a feeling of authority. For example, many teaching assistants start by imitating favorite teachers of their own. As you get more experience and confidence, you will be able to act more natural in your role as an instructor. You then will be able to be more yourself while being a teacher.

> "As a college student, I was taught by a teaching assistant who looked like she was thirteen years old. Although she looked so young, her confidence, competence, and terrific preparation for class earned everybody's respect by the end of the first meeting."

The Joys of Teaching

While teaching is an additional burden for already busy graduate students, there are several significant pleasures to being a teacher.

Giving Back

Teaching allows you to help other students learn and grow. It also reminds you that you already have a great deal to contribute to the teaching in your field, even if you still have a long way to go in your own education. You spend a lot of your time as a student focused on what you don't know; teaching helps you remember how much you do know.

Improving Your Own Studies

Teaching helps you to be a better student. You will become more receptive to the efforts of your own professors after you have sat on the other side of the desk. Teaching also makes you learn material more thoroughly than you ever learned it as a student.

Preparing for Your Career

Teaching as a graduate student offers excellent training to those who will go on to become professional teachers. It helps you become comfortable in the classroom and find your own teaching style.

Expanding Your World

The life of a graduate student can be startlingly narrow. Many graduate students find that most of their time is spent doing very focused research and interacting with a relatively small number of colleagues. Teaching allows you to meet people at the university who are not your classmates or your professors. In addition, it can be a pleasure to feel that you are gainfully employed, even while you are pursuing your own course of studies.

Enjoying the Job

Teaching can be fun in and of itself. It allows you to be creative and enthusiastic. The chance to explore material in your field and your students' curiosity can also fuel your enthusiasm about your own research and your field in general.

The Agonies of Teaching

At some point in your teaching career, you will fall flat on your face. It will probably happen more than once. It may be painful, but you will survive. And you should find it reassuring to know that *every* instructor has had this happen.

Bad Days

You can come to class feeling completely prepared to teach brilliantly and leave wishing you had never gotten out of bed. See if you can figure out what went wrong. Keep notes; you might teach the same course again several years later, and you usually know what you could have done better as soon as you leave the classroom. Learn from this experience but do not torture yourself about it. Focus on making the next class better.

See chapter 9, "Meta-teaching," for more information on what to do after a bad day.

Bad Courses

This happens. Some classes never gel; the professor organizes the course poorly; the course tries to cover too much or too difficult material; you are not doing your best teaching for personal reasons. It is unfortunate when this happens, and all that you can do is figure out what went wrong and how you can teach the course better the next time.

Bad Class Dynamics

Any teaching assistant with more than one section at a time can attest that some sections work well and some do not. Your first reaction may be to blame yourself when a section does not go well but also remember that the students play a key role in an effective classroom too. It may help to try adjusting your teaching style to a particular group of students, but there will be groups of students who never come together.

Bad Teaching

Your car broke down. A relationship ended. You were up until 3:00 A.M. grading. You have had five cups of coffee, and you *cannot* wake up. You will have bad days. It is your responsibility to do your best not to let outside factors bring down your teaching. When you teach badly, figure out how you can take care of yourself so that you are in better shape when it is time to teach again. Obsessing about what went wrong will not get you on the road to feeling (and teaching) better.

Maintaining Perspective

If you take teaching seriously, it can become almost life consuming. Class preparation and grading can take up as much time as you allow them. And you can wrap up too much of your self-image in your performance as an instructor. A good teaching day can put you on an affirming high, and a bad teaching day can ruin your week. Cherish the highs (they can be a rare treat in graduate school) and focus on reacting productively to the lows.

What Your Students Are Thinking after Class

While you may spend the rest of the week fretting over whether or not your discussion was as lively as last week or whether the diagram you drew on the board was confusing, your students are not worrying about your class as much as you are. Most students are more focused on grasping the content of the material than on observing how you teach it. Additionally, undergraduates also have many other things on their minds besides your course (e.g., the exam they have that afternoon, their attraction to another student in your class). Some students will think about the class after they leave, but if the class did not go well, they may be as likely to attribute responsibility to themselves or to their classmates as they are to you. Try to remember this when you find yourself overly worried about how the class is working.

> "One night at the supermarket, I wheeled my cart into the check-out line right behind one of my students. She looked completely shocked. She clearly believed that I did not exist outside the classroom."

What You Should Be Thinking after Class

An important part of teaching is learning from experience. When a class goes well, think about what went right so that you can repeat it. When a class goes badly, think about what went wrong but do not kick yourself about it; just fix it. See it as a learning experience, not as a statement about your ultimate abilities as a teacher. Most mistakes can be fixed in the next class, and remember that a bad class session does not make a bad course.

Care about your students and their learning. Also be kind to yourself and remember you're still learning too.

Further Reading

Allen, R. R., and T. Rueter. 1990. *Teaching Assistant Strategies*. Dubuque, IA: Kendall/Hunt.

Davis, B. G. 1993. *Tools for Teaching*. San Francisco: Jossey-Bass.

Eble, K. 1988. *The Craft of Teaching*. 2d ed. San Francisco: Jossey-Bass.

Lambert, L. M., S. L. Tice, and P. H. Featherstone, eds. 1996. *University Teaching: A Guide for Graduate Students*. Syracuse, NY: Syracuse University Press.

McKeachie, W. J., and M. Svinicki. 2006. *McKeachie's Teaching Tips: Strategies, Research, and Theory for College and University Teachers*. 12th ed. Boston: Houghton Mifflin.

Zanna, M. P., and J. M. Darley, eds. 1987. *The Compleat Academic: A Practical Guide for the Beginning Social Scientist*. New York: Random House.

Chapter 2
The First Day of the Term

The first day of teaching, whether it is your first day ever or just the first day of the term, is a simultaneously exhilarating and terrifying experience. You do not know the students, and you want to make a good first impression. You may not be sure of the course logistics, yet you want to sound like you are. This chapter will help you plan for and survive your first day with as little stress as possible.

> "I think the day I stop getting nervous before the first day of class—and even a little nervous and 'adrenalined' before every class—may be the day I become a less good teacher."

Before Classes Begin

Here is a short checklist to help you avoid many "first day" headaches.

Know Your Students

If you can get the class list ahead of time, begin to familiarize yourself with the students' names. You will have an easier time remembering names if you already have a sense of them. If you cannot get a class list in advance, find out how many students you should expect so that you will know how many chairs you will need and how many copies of handouts to make.

Some universities now have a facebook, so you can see students' photos with the class list. If you want to, you can also check www.face book.com, and you will probably find photos of many of your students. Photos can really help in learning names.

Check Your Classroom

Look at the classroom before your first class meeting. First of all, you want to be sure you know where it is. Getting lost on the way to class can take all of the fun out of your first day of teaching. Second, you need to know how the chairs are arranged and whether they can be moved; where the board is and whether it comes with chalk, pens, and an eraser; whether there is a table or podium, and so on. This way, you can be realistic when you think about the logistics of the first day. And you can be sure to have at least as many chairs as you have students.

Check Class Start Times

At some universities, classes actually begin ten (or more) minutes after the time printed in the course schedule to allow students time to get from one class to the next. Check to see if such a policy exists at your university.

Meet the Administrative Staff

Find out which administrator is responsible for the teaching of under-graduates in your department and make a point of meeting them and their staff. It will prove immensely useful later in the term if you know and are on friendly terms with the director of undergraduate studies, the supervisor of all of the chemistry labs, or the coordinator of the introductory language program. You may look to this person for advice or intervention in a difficult situation, and it helps if they already know who you are.

Administrative assistants in the department wield much of the bureaucratic clout, so (common decency aside) you would do well to be polite and friendly in your interactions with them. These people can often make a room change, an equipment loan, or another teaching request proceed quickly and smoothly if you ask nicely. They also are often the source of invaluable advice.

Develop Your Class Plan

Create a detailed class plan. The more detail you put into the plan, the more confident you will feel walking into the classroom. Think about what you are going to say at the start of class and practice it in front of a mirror. It sounds silly to practice your opening, but you have a better shot at delivering it effectively if you have done it before.

See chapter 3, "The Lesson Plan," for more information on writing lesson plans.

Do Your Copying

Make copies of all the syllabi and handouts that you will need. Do not leave this task until the day of your first class because there are always a lot of people making copies at the start of the term. There either will be a huge line or the copier will have gotten tired and decided to stop working.

Know the Drop/Add Policy

Find out about your department's policy for adding students to a class or section. Do you have the authority to add students to an already full class? If students do not come to the first day or two of class, can you (or must you) drop them from the class? How do you drop and add students from the class? How should you handle a wait list?

Organize Yourself

Decide what you're going to wear and make sure it's clean (and ironed if need be!). Pack your bag with everything you will need:

- copies of the course syllabus,
- copies of all other handouts,
- lesson plan,
- class list,
- grade book,
- pens and pencils,
- chalk pens and eraser (if needed),
- index cards for student information,
- a watch or a cell phone with a clock.

Outfitting Yourself

What you wear and the accoutrements you bring will affect how you feel about yourself as a teacher and how your students view you.

Teaching Clothes

Unlike many jobs, teaching at a university gives you more flexibility in the formality of your attire. Your clothes should always be clean, well kept, and of appropriate "coverage," but their style is a personal choice.

Dressing Up

PROS   Students can see that you take your job seriously.

You look and may feel more professional.

You may have less trouble establishing your authority in the classroom.

You create a distinction between your teaching job and your student life.

You give your students something nice to look at.

CONS   It creates more sense of distance between you and your students (this could also be a "pro").

You may not be as comfortable in these clothes.

Nice clothes can be expensive.

Dressing Down

PROS   You may be very comfortable in these clothes.

You probably already own these clothes.

It may make students feel more comfortable approaching you.

CONS   Students may take you less seriously as a teacher.

Students may be more likely to question your authority.

You may feel less put together.

Outer Wear

If you can leave your coat, hat, umbrella, and so on, in your office before class, do so. It gives you less to keep track of going into and leaving class. If this is not possible, think about where you want to remove your outdoor gear (in front of the class, in the back of the classroom, in the hall, etc.), especially if it involves pulling a coat over your head.

Bags

Shoulder bags are a popular choice among teaching assistants because they look professional, but a good-looking backpack works as well if you prefer it. You may want to bring the bag to class because it is an easy way to carry papers, pens, and so forth. Unloading your bag in your office and bringing only the class material you need to the classroom is also an efficient way of organizing yourself before class and making sure that you really do have everything you need.

Introducing Yourself

Many teaching assistants worry that they are ill equipped for teaching if they are barely removed from the undergraduate experience themselves. While you may feel that you have little to offer your students that they cannot offer each other, you will quickly discover that, in fact, you do know much more than they do about your area of study. Remember that your students walk in expecting you to know more, and it is your job on the first day to establish your legitimacy as their teacher.

Your Name

On the first day, you should let your students know what you want to be called; you may want to put your name on the board so that they can see what you want to be called. Many teaching assistants opt to be called by their first name, but using Mr. or Ms. is also a sensible option. To some extent, your decision will affect the formality of your relationship with the students. Do what feels most comfortable for you.

It can be very awkward for students if they do not know how to address you, both in person and on e-mail. Some will default to "Professor _____ ," which you will have to correct (many undergraduates are not aware of the distinctions among levels of faculty and instructional staff). Others will wait for eye contact to begin speaking rather than addressing you. Others may opt for "Hey!" You facilitate easier communication from the get-go by establishing how you would like to be addressed.

Your Background

Fundamentally, most of your students assume you are qualified and do not necessarily care too much about your official qualifications as a teacher. What they do care about is your interest in and knowledge of the subject you are teaching. The more enthusiastic you are about the course, the more enthusiastic you can expect your students to be. Speak briefly, if at all, about your undergraduate education or experience in your field but do not belabor this subject (as we said, they don't necessarily care). Some of your previous experiences will also emerge naturally in discussions throughout the term.

There is no reason to discuss your age or the age difference between you and your students unless, for some reason, it becomes relevant. The same is true for other aspects of your personal life; if they see a wedding ring, they will figure out its significance, but outside of that, there is no reason to divulge the details of your personal life, your sexual orientation, and so on, unless you feel this information is relevant to the class.

If they do ask a personal question, you are free to indicate that this question is not relevant, important, or appropriate. You might deal with this humorously ("Actually, I am a very young-looking 89!") or directly ("Right now I am only addressing questions relevant to the course."). Do not worry that you are "blowing the student off." What you are doing is maintaining appropriate student-teacher boundaries and helping students to learn what sorts of questions *are* appropriate for class.

Remember: you can always tell your students more about yourself as the semester progresses, but you cannot take back anything you say on the first day.

Your Gender

Issues of gender are subtle, complex, and extremely powerful, and they are at work in every classroom. When you are thinking about introducing yourself to your students, do not forget that they are also meeting you as their new male or female teacher.

Your gender will influence the power dynamic between you and your students, and it will also influence the power dynamic among your students. While this can be a good thing (e.g., female teachers in the sciences may inspire undergraduate women to consider graduate school) there are an infinite number of ways that the power dynamic in a classroom may be disrupted by issues related to gender.

- Male *and* female students may be less inclined to respect the authority of female teachers.

- Female students may be more or less inclined to speak in a class taught by a man; male students may say more or less in front of female teachers.

- Male students may aim to intimidate female teachers; male teachers may intimidate female students.

- Teachers may be overly flirtatious with their students; students may be overly flirtatious with their teachers.

- Female teachers may be less respected in some fields (e.g., physics), while male teachers may be less respected in others (e.g., social work).

Regardless of your gender, you should keep in mind that gender dynamics are also at work among the students themselves. Unless you are teaching a class about gender, it is unlikely that you will need or want to make an explicit issue of the gender-related power dynamics in your classroom. However, such issues should be on your mind now and throughout the semester. There are many subtle ways that you can manage gender-related issues in your classroom.

- Be sure that men and women are equal participants in class discussions; if they are not, consider possible reasons for this and make the necessary changes.

- Be nonsexist in your presentation of material (e.g., using both males and females in your examples).

- Demonstrate that you expect to be respected regardless of your gender by treating all of your students with equal respect.

- While students may come to the class with sexist ideas about male or female teachers, they will almost always respond to a teacher's command of the material, regardless of their gender.

Your Race and Culture

Like issues related to gender, issues related to race and culture are extremely powerful within the classroom. Almost everything noted previously about gender applies to issues of race and culture.

- Students may be less inclined to respect the authority of minority teachers.

- Depending on the teacher's race or culture, minority students or students who are members of the dominant culture may feel less inclined to speak in class.

- Both students and teachers may exploit the power differential that exists among different racial and ethnic groups.

- Regardless of *your* race or culture, race and culture dynamics will be at work among your students.

In addition to those noted earlier, there are some special issues that arise with regard to race and culture.

- While your gender is typically obvious to your students, your race and culture may not be.

- You may not be able to identify your students' racial and cultural backgrounds.

- Racism may result from ignorance—there are many college students who meet people from certain racial or cultural backgrounds for the first time in college; sexism rarely results from similar ignorance—most college students have had ample contact with competent men and women.

Again, unless you are teaching a course on racial or cultural issues, you may not need or want to make racial and cultural difference an explicit issue in your classroom. As with issues related to gender, the power of racial and cultural differences should be on your mind throughout the semester. You should use your position of authority to make sure that all students are treated respectfully by you and their classmates and that everyone in your classroom has an equal voice. If you suspect that potentially offensive behavior is a result of ignorance, use your role as a teacher to provide students with important information. For example, you might try to catch a student after class or write a note on their paper letting them know that most Native Americans prefer not to be referred to as "Indians."

See chapter 4, "Handling Sensitive Material" for more information on addressing sensitive issues in class.

Your Language

Teaching assistants who are nonnative English speakers, whether they were born in the United States or abroad, face a different set of challenges in the classroom, sometimes due to real language barriers and sometimes due to student assumptions and/or biases. Students often complain about "foreign TAs" (in nonforeign language classes), and they often judge foreignness by accent.

In most cases, accent differences should not be a problem for you or your students. Indeed, many undergraduates welcome the opportunity to learn from someone from another country. But, you may also discover that some students respond negatively to a foreign accent. At times, some students will transfer their frustration with the material to frustration with your accent. Regardless of the prejudices students have at the beginning of the semester, they will typically respond positively to your competence in and enthusiasm for the field.

You may want to start the term by telling your students where you are from and whatever else about your background you deem appropriate. If you feel that your accent is noticeable, you can acknowledge that and tell your students that they will quickly become accustomed to your speech. Encourage them to ask questions if they ever have trouble understanding what you are saying.

EXAMPLE   "I know that my accent may be unfamiliar—if you are having any trouble understanding me now, you will become accustomed to my speech after a couple of classes. Please feel free to stop me and ask to me to repeat anything I say that you do not understand—it will not be a problem."

At almost all universities, you will have passed an English exam that qualifies you to teach in a U.S. classroom. However, if you find that there is a real language barrier in your classroom, that your students cannot understand your presentation of the material and/or you cannot understand their questions, it is your responsibility to seek help. Contact your university's resource center for international graduate students or seek out published material for international graduate student teachers. Do not feel that a language barrier speaks to your qualifications as a teacher generally; just be sure that you are taking the necessary steps to teach effectively in a predominantly English-speaking classroom.

Establishing Contact

Be clear about how and when students can reach you. Give all this information to students *in writing* on the first day, either on the board or on the syllabus.

E-mail

With e-mail, your students can contact you at any hour without even interrupting you. You may want to encourage students to use e-mail as a way to ask questions about assignments, make appointments, or even talk about issues that arise in class. Be clear with your students about how often you check e-mail and how promptly they can expect a response.

E-mail cannot (and should not) replace the one-on-one interaction possible during office hours. If a student's questions are too numerous and/or far reaching to be answered appropriately on e-mail, or if you feel the student will learn more from a conversation with you, use your e-mail response to make an appointment with the student to visit you during office hours.

> "It's midnight the night before the paper is due, and the phone rings. Why I answered it, I don't know—I knew it had to be a student. 'I think I lost the assignment sheet,' she said plaintively. 'Can you read it to me so that I can write it down?' That was the last time I gave out my home phone! E-mail never wakes me up."

Office Phone Number

If your department provides an office where you can be reached or where students can leave messages, give this number to students (with warnings about how quickly the message will get to you).

Home or Cell Phone Number

Giving students your home or cell phone number can be problematic because you may hear from them at inappropriate times and more often than you might wish. If you choose to give students your number, you should give them clear guidelines about what hours they may call. Do not expect that they will respect these guidelines. In general, we do not recommend giving students your home or cell phone number.

> **SAMPLE SYLLABUS HEADING**
>
> Philosophy 234 (Modern German Philosophy), Section 3
> MW 1:00–2:30
>
> Joe Schmo, Instructor
> Office: K-411 Concrete Hall
> Office Phone: 555–4242 (8 AM – 5 PM, leave a message with the secretary)
> Office Hours: W 2:30–4:00
>   Th 9:00–10:00 (and by appointment)
> E-mail: schmo@univ.edu (I am on the system M – F 8 AM – 6 PM, so this is an
>   easy way to ask questions, make an appointment, etc.)

Class E-mail Groups

Now that almost all students have and use e-mail regularly, you may want to set up a class e-mail group. You can use this to send messages to the entire class, and students can use it to get in touch with each other. Many universities also now offer course-based web sites where you can post announcements as well as class materials. If you will be sending timely messages through the e-mail group (e.g., assignment updates) or posting them on the web site, you must be sure to remind students to check their mail on the web site frequently. Set a policy about what constitutes appropriate e-mail to this list (e.g., "no keggers announced here").

Office Hours

Most departments require teaching assistants to hold one to three office hours a week. Try to schedule your hours at a time that is convenient for your students and for you and be sure to let them know that you can schedule other meeting times if they cannot attend office hours. While it may be tempting to schedule office hours only at your convenience, in the end, you will save yourself time and trouble and, more importantly, be a better teacher by being more readily accessible to your students. That said, schedule office hours in a way that also makes sense with your schedule. If Tuesdays are free, perhaps you don't want to schedule office hours right in the middle of the day. It can work well to schedule office hours adjacent to other commitments you have on campus.

See chapter 7, "Office Hours," for more information on holding office hours.

Meeting before and after Class

Students often will expect to be able to grab you after class for a brief consultation, and if they can, there is no need to say anything. But if you are on a tight schedule, you should let students know that you will not be available immediately before or after class and that they should plan on arranging a different time to talk to you (office hours, by e-mail, etc.).

Syllabus: Setting the Agenda

Use the syllabus as a kind of contract with your students. It outlines what you expect from your students and what your students can expect in return. As with a legal document, the more specific and detailed you make the policies on the syllabus, the easier they will be to "enforce." If you are leading a discussion section for a lecture course, the professor will have provided a syllabus, but you may want to supplement this with your own.

Establishing Policies

Be as detailed as you possibly can with all of your policies about attendance, late work, missed exams, and so on. You will be glad to have these guidelines to follow if/when these issues arise. For example, be specific about how much grades will be lowered for each day an assignment is late or for a missed lab. Part of your job is to establish your authority as a teacher, and having clear policies indicates to your students that you are comfortable in this role.

Setting the Tone for the Semester

The entire syllabus does not have to be seriously worded. You can be amusing but firm about issues like attendance and class participation. Remember: you are letting students get a sense of who you are and how you expect to relate to them. The paragraph on plagiarism, however, should be nothing but serious.

Do not worry about being too strict or sounding too firm about the rules on the first day. As long as your policies are fair, they are beneficial to everyone. Remember: you can always ease up on the rules later in the term but it is extremely difficult to become more strict in a way that will seem credible to your students. Students appreciate knowing the rules and the penalties for violating them.

What to Include

The syllabus is the students' reference sheet for the course, so include as much pertinent information as you can. That said, a syllabus should not become novel-like in length or get overly chatty. Decide what absolutely needs to be on the syllabus and what related explanations you can go over orally in class.

Required or Highly Recommended Information

The following information should be presented clearly on the syllabus:

- all of your "bureaucratic" information: name, office location and hours, office phone number, e-mail address;

- required texts and where to purchase them;

- any and all deadlines for assignments and dates for exams;

- a breakdown by points or percentages for how much all work and class participation count toward the final grade;

- attendance policy: how many absences students are allowed and how further absences will affect their grade (also know the university's policies on religious holidays and students traveling for university-sponsored activities such as athletics—but these may not need to go on the syllabus);

- policy on late work and missed exams;

- information about how students with learning disabilities or other special needs can request special accommodations;

- the university's policy on plagiarism (it is important to go over this in detail with students, given the usually serious consequences for violating the policy).

   See chapter 7, "Plagiarism," for more information on dealing with plagiarism.

Optional Information

Some of the following information may be more appropriate in some classes than others, and much of it can be presented in other forms or forums, rather than on the syllabus itself:

- the course description;

- course goals or objectives;

- weekly schedule with topics and readings (some instructors provide the schedule in two parts if they have not yet determined what material will need to be covered in the second half of the term);

- brief descriptions of required assignments;

- a brief description of what you mean by class participation;

- classroom conduct policies: cell phones and beepers, food and drink, e-mail etiquette;

- course advice: study tips, note-taking, group work, availability of tutors or other resources;

- ways that students can provide you with feedback about the course. *See appendix A for a sample syllabus.*

The First Class Meeting

The first day of class can set the tone for the term. If you want students to participate during the term, they should participate on the first day.

Do not expect to teach too much content on the first day that your class meets, but try to include some substantive activity. Your main goal is to interest the students in the course and give them a sense of the kinds of issues, questions, and skills the course will address. The other tasks include taking attendance, beginning to learn names, filling out information cards, and going over the syllabus. If you are teaching a science lab, you may use the first day of class to introduce students to the lab and to review safety procedures. We highly recommend not dismissing class early, even though students may come with that expectation. It is a good idea for them to become used to being in class for the full time right from the start. If you think that you won't have enough material to fill all of the class time, consider some of the icebreakers offered later in this chapter.

Making Your Entrance

Your students will invariably stop talking and stare at you the moment you enter the classroom. You may find that on the first day you want to arrive right on time because you do not know your students' names and you want to avoid this awkward silence. As the semester progresses, you may want to come early to deal with bureaucratic details or to chat with students.

Arriving a Few Minutes Early

PRO   You have time to get organized, arrange chairs, erase the board, talk to students about class assignments, enjoy informal "classroom banter."

CON   You may have to suffer the unbearable silence of sitting with the two or three students who have trickled in early and who will not speak to each other in your presence (and who may feel awkward speaking with you).

Arriving Exactly on Time

PRO   This makes the beginning of class a more clear-cut event (class begins when you arrive), and it avoids the awkwardness of silent dead time before class.

CON   You need to be completely organized before you walk in the door, or you will be forced to start class late. Therefore, you may want to take all of the materials that you will be using during class out of your bag and carry them into the room so that you do not have to unpack your bag while students wait and watch.

> "I am compulsively early, and so on the first day of class, I arrived in the classroom ten minutes early. There were three students there who stopped talking when they realized I was the teacher. I had no idea who they were or what to say to them, so we said nothing, which meant that every new student who entered the room became deathly silent when they came in. It was a mean feat to revive that class when those awful ten minutes were finally over."

Taking Attendance

Write your name and the course name and number on the board so that any students who have suddenly found themselves in the wrong classroom can leave. After you introduce yourself and give as much background as you see fit, you probably will want to go over the class list to see who is and is not there. Be sure to ask students to correct your pronunciation of their names and to tell you if they prefer to be called by something other than their given name. Get the names of any students present in the class who are not on the list and tell them their status for getting in (or ask to see them after class). Remind all the students of your drop/add policy; for example, they may need to attend the second meeting in order not to be dropped from the class.

In future class sessions, you can take attendance by passing around a sign-up sheet, or you can simply mark down who is absent once you know all their names.

Learning Names

Learn your students' names as quickly as you can. No excuses allowed here (e.g., "I'm just not good at names"). Focus on it and you'll be able to do it. You have memorized many more arduous things in your career. It makes an enormous difference with students and the whole class dynamic for you to refer to them by name. Some instructors make notes on their roster to help them remember which students go with which names (e.g., buzz cut, nose ring).

Information Cards

Having a note card with each student's "vital information" can prove invaluable later in the term if you need to get in touch with them. Write on the board (inside a re-creation of a card if you're feeling artistic) all the information you would like them to include. The crucial items: name, address, phone number, e-mail address. Optional items: their major, interests, expectations of the course, other courses that term, and so forth.

NAME:	YEAR:
MAJOR:	PHONE #:
E-MAIL:	
INTERESTS IN THIS AREA:	
REASONS FOR TAKING THE CLASS:	
OTHER COURSES THIS SEMESTER:	

Icebreakers

You may want to try these icebreakers before you go over the syllabus because they can begin to establish a sense of unity in the class. They are a way for you to learn students' names and to get a better sense of the makeup of the class. Also, if you want students to learn each other's names, you must give them a way to meet each other.

Introducing Your Icebreaker

Many students and teaching assistants find any icebreaker to be a painfully corny exercise. They're right. However, icebreakers usually do "break the ice," and students will be more willing to participate in your icebreaker if you acknowledge from the beginning that the task is a corny one while giving your reasons for doing it anyway.

EXAMPLE   "I know that your worst fear about the first day of class is about to be realized, and that exercises like this can seem really silly, but I have found that this is the quickest way for all of us to meet and learn a bit about each other."

Sample Icebreakers

Introducing a Partner

1. Have the students pair up with someone they do not know and give each pair a total of four minutes to interview each other. (If you have an odd number of students, have one group include three students.)

2. Tell them that they only need to get basic information such as each other's name, year in college, hometown, and interests. You can also have students find out why their classmates are interested in this course and/or tell each other something particularly memorable about themselves.

3. Watch the time for them and make sure that they switch roles (from interviewer to interviewee) after two minutes.

4. Give each student about one minute to introduce their partner.

You don't need to participate because you already have introduced yourself. This icebreaker relieves students of the pressure of having to talk about themselves in front of an unfamiliar group, and, by the time you are finished, each student should feel familiar with at least one other person in the class.

Introducing Oneself

Go around the room and have each student give their name and year in college. In addition, ask each student to tell the class at least one interesting fact about themselves (or one thing that makes them unique or particularly memorable). You can set the tone of this icebreaker (which can be quite humorous) by going first. For example you might share that you were given an F in singing as a kindergartner or some equally silly tidbit. Or you can ask each student to find a random item in their backpack and explain its significance. As students introduce themselves, you can create a student "map" on the board that you all can use later in the class as you try to remember names. This icebreaker takes less time than the first one, and if you start with some humor, students won't feel too painfully "on the spot."

Reviewing the Syllabus

It is not enough to hand out the syllabus and expect students to read it. They may not. But you don't have to read it to them either. Have students read various key paragraphs in the syllabus aloud. Call on one student to read the first key paragraph (this also can be a good way to learn names). After they finish, you can emphasize important points or add any supplemental information (make these notes to yourself beforehand on your syllabus because once you are in class, you may not remember the things that seemed important to you the night before). For the next paragraph, you can either call on another student or have the first student choose a classmate to pick up where they left off (this way, they have to start learning each other's names).

You should review your attendance policy, your grading policy, late assignment policy, and the university's rules on plagiarism. The clearer you are about this off the bat, the fewer hassles you will run into later (and if these hassles do arise, you have covered yourself).

You do not have to review the syllabus first thing. You can include a content-based activity on the first day and then go over the syllabus near the end of class.

Using up Remaining Time

You may want to come prepared with at least one exercise you can use if you have time remaining at the end of class. You can give a brief introductory lecture if you feel comfortable doing so. You also can learn more about the makeup of your class by asking your students an "introductory question."

EXAMPLES   "Have you ever felt math anxiety? When?"
           "Can people tell where you're from by the way you speak? What do they say?"
           "What do you see as your strengths and weaknesses as a writer?"
           "Why are you taking this course?"

You can ask students to share their thoughts aloud, either with the full class or in small groups, or you can have them spend five to ten minutes writing in response to the question. You can collect these papers and use them to get a better sense of who your students are and what they know. This material also may work well as an introduction to the next class.

Further Reading

Davis, B. G. 1993. *Tools for Teaching*. San Francisco: Jossey-Bass.

Filene, P. 2005. *The Joy of Teaching: A Practical Guide for New College Instructors*. Chapel Hill: University of North Carolina Press.

Geismar, K., and G. Nicoleau, eds. 1993. *Teaching for Change: Addressing Issues of Difference in the College Classroom*. Cambridge, MA: Harvard Educational Review.

Lambert, L. M., S. L. Tice, and P. H. Featherstone, eds. 1996. *University Teaching: A Guide for Graduate Students*. Syracuse, NY: Syracuse University Press.

Lie, S. S., and V. O'Leary, eds. 1990. *Storming the Tower: Women in the Academic World*. East Brunswick, NJ: Nichols/GP.

McKeachie, W. J., and M. Svinicki. 2006. *McKeachie's Teaching Tips: Strategies, Research, and Theory for College and University Teachers*. 12th ed. Boston: Houghton Mifflin.

Provitera-McGlynn, A. 2001. *Successful Beginnings for College Teaching: Engaging Your Students from the First Day*. Madison: Atwood Publishing.

Ryan, M. P. 1989. *Planning a College Course: A Guidebook for the Graduate Teaching Assistant.* Ann Arbor, MI: National Center for Research to Improve Postsecondary Teaching and Learning.

Smith, J. 1992. *Communicate: Strategies for International Teaching Assistants.* Englewood Cliffs, NJ: Regents/Prentice Hall.

Chapter 3
Weekly Class Preparation

Even the most experienced teachers need to plan what they will do in every class. This chapter details the steps involved in developing an organized and meaningful lesson plan.

The Goal of the Class

Most teaching assistants meet with their students for about one hour, and rarely for more than three hours, each week (labs, of course, are longer). Your job is to use your teaching time to make learning happen. This can occur in many ways. You might impart factual information to your students, help them to clarify and consolidate information that was already presented to them in lecture, encourage them to see old information in new ways, or provide hands-on experience for a concept covered in lecture. Regardless of your approach, your students should know more, understand more, or have something new to think about by the time they pack their bags to head off to their next class.

Having a Goal

You will be most effective as a teacher if you focus your energies on meeting one or two major goals in a given session. Our first instinct can be to focus purely on the content we hope to cover. We encourage you to begin by articulating for yourself what you would say if a colleague stopped you in the hall after class and asked, "What did your students gain in class today?" The answer will be the learning goals that should then drive your decisions about the content you will cover. These goals may be focused on students mastering specific material, grasping broad intellectual questions or approaches that underlie the material, or developing particular analytic skills.

In terms of class content, home in on the areas that will help you achieve your class goals. Be sure to share with your students the goals behind that day's class content and activities. The key is that students will have an easier time grasping the material if it is clearly related, focused, and contextualized. If they know what it is that they are trying to gain from a particular class, they will be able to gauge their success and ask better questions.

"A lesson plan? You mean I was supposed to have one of those?"

EXAMPLES   *Goal:* Help students adopt the appropriate convention for scientific writing by reviewing the proper format for a lab report.
Lesson: Hand out sample lab reports to class; point out to students the strengths and weaknesses of each. Invite their comments and questions.

Goal: Develop the students' capacity to consider controversial issues from multiple perspectives by providing a forum in which students challenge their own ideas about the legalization of marijuana.
Lesson: Organize a debate in which every student is required to argue both sides of the issue.

Goal: Foster the students' understanding of how political climates shape the response to political crises by examining the circumstances surrounding the Bay of Pigs crisis.
Lesson: Have students read through the correspondence between Kennedy's advisers before class; divide them into groups at the beginning of class and have each group summarize the position of a particular adviser; have each group present its summary to the rest of the class; have the entire class assess the various advisers' points.

Prioritizing Goals

Sometimes you will have a long list of points to cover. In this case, be sure to prioritize your goals and start with the one that is most critical to helping your students understand class material. If you get through the first concept quickly, move on to the next one. Think carefully about how to create a transition between points so that students understand how the material fits together. Always remember that the material is much newer to them than it is to you and they may not see connections as easily as you do.

"The best analogy I have ever heard about teaching involves books and bookshelves. The concepts in our field are like books. When we teach the concepts, we are giving students books. The key to good teaching is to remember that they may not have a bookshelf on which to put the books. We need to give them books, help them build the bookshelf, and then help them organize the books on the bookshelf."

The Lesson Plan

Once you have established your teaching goal(s) for a particular class, *write it down*. You must be very clear with yourself about what you are trying to teach. Once you have written down your goal(s), sketch a plan to make the relevant concepts accessible and interesting to your students. Before you start writing your lesson plan, make the following decisions.

- How much talking will you do, and what will you talk about?

- How much will you expect your students to participate?

- What relevant activities can help you make your point?

- Will your students need to prepare for the class meeting in advance?

If your students will need to do special preparation in advance of your class meeting, be sure to let them know one week ahead of time so that they have fair warning. This means that you will have to be one week ahead of your students in your lesson plans.

Writing a Lesson Plan

Although it may seem silly and tedious, you should write down everything that you plan to do in your teaching time. While you may have a very clear plan outlined in your head, it is easy to forget important details once you are faced with the questions and concerns of twenty or more students. This can be especially important in lab classes when reminding students of critical details may make a difference in the outcome of their experiments.

Most teaching assistants use an outline format for their lesson plans. This makes it easier for you to know where you are and where you are headed when you glance at the plan during class. You may even want to color code parts of your lesson plan so that you can find your place quickly when class gets rolling.

Telling Students the Plan

When you have spent so much time creating your lesson plan, it can be easy to forget that your students come to class with no idea about what you are planning to do. At the beginning of class, give them an overview or brief outline of the plan for the day, including the goals. Classroom activities can work exponentially better when students know how the class time will be spent and understand why they are doing what they are doing.

Facilitating Student Notes

Some students learn and study effectively from well-organized notes, and the organization of their notes depends on your providing structure to the information. If you are lecturing, you may want to put an outline of the major points on the board so that students know where you are going. You can then check them off as you cover them. You can also write the major points on the board as you go. As you speak, highlight and review the main points so that students can see how they are related and which ideas are subordinate to others.

- Use the board as much as you can. Students know that what you write on the board is important. It also slows you down, which gives students time to write down information. If you elect to use PowerPoint, be sure to limit the words on each slide and allow students plenty of time to copy slide content.

- Use numbers so that students know how many points you are making and can organize their notes accordingly (e.g., "There are three kinds of insect life in this river. The first . . .").

Incorporating Writing

Asking students to write about course material requires them to think through and to fully articulate their ideas. In written assignments, you and your students can get a clearer sense of what they understand and where they are still struggling. Writing can also be an opportunity for students to build an academic argument in a systematic, detailed, and appropriately supported manner. We encourage you to consider incorporating writing assignments in all disciplines, including the natural sciences. By writing, students move immediately from passively receiving information to actively synthesizing ideas and creating original arguments.

Students can often learn more about writing in your discipline and about the topic of the paper when given assignments that include submitting a proposal (and getting feedback), writing a draft (and getting feedback), and revising to create the final version of the paper. As you can tell from this description, students need and will benefit from your guidance as they master the expected conventions for a formal paper's content and format within your discipline. Students can learn much more from working through, step by step, the stages involved in getting one paper "right" than from writing three different papers.

Allotting Time

You should guesstimate how long each part of your lesson plan will take and allot your class time so that you will be able to cover all of the necessary material. You can write down the number of minutes allowed for each part of the lesson plan or the time at which you expect to begin an activity so that you do not run out of time at the end. Be sure to leave time to wrap up the class and review relevant points. Even though you may have taught with utter clarity and precision, students still will benefit from a brief summary of what just happened in class.

You do not want so strict a lesson plan as to "run over" student questions, but you also do not want to get bogged down in minor issues when major points still desperately need attention. It will help if you have some material near the end of the lesson plan that you see as optional or that you can bump into the next class session. This way you will have the flexibility to dwell longer on a topic that turns out to be of particular interest or concern to students. At the same time, use your judgment and authority to bring closure to a discussion you see as no longer productive or relevant and to steer the students back toward the major topics of the class.

EXAMPLE   "There are so many interesting aspects to this topic, I wish we had time to pursue them all. Let's get back to the core of what we're dealing with today."

Bureaucratic Details

Although bureaucratic matters are not part of your formal lesson for the day, you will want to add them to your lesson plan. This will include things like making plans to talk with individual students, announcing a change in your office hours, scheduling review sessions, or telling students when they will get back graded material. This is also a time to solicit student questions about bureaucratic matters that may be relevant to the entire class.

You will usually want to attend to these items before you move into your lesson for the day, and they are likely to be issues that students come to class concerned about. At the end of the class students have often already shut their notebooks or you have run out of time. And trust us, you want to write these details down—they will be the first things that you forget once you walk into the classroom.

Lesson Format

Most courses taught by graduate students use one of three (broadly defined) teaching formats: more loosely planned discussion sections, lectures, and more highly structured classes that include preplanned student activities. Decide on which one you will use for a particular class and then develop your lesson plan accordingly.

Even if the material you are teaching is traditionally presented in a lecture format (and this is how it was presented to you as an undergraduate), do not feel that lecturing is your only option. Almost all lessons can be adapted to a variety of formats; you can transmit a great deal of information while involving your students.

Whatever format you choose for a particular lesson, do not use the same format for every class. Vary your lesson plans from week to week, not only to keep things lively but also to make sure you are reaching students with different learning styles.

Different students learn well in different ways. Some students can take organized lecture notes and absorb the material; others need more active engagement with the material to grasp it. Some students can listen and learn; others are more visually oriented. By mixing up your lesson plans and providing material in different media, you facilitate learning for all students and help them become accustomed to learning material in different ways.

Discussion Classes

If you will be running a discussion, you need to determine your goal(s) for the discussion. Then think through and write out the questions that you will use to get the discussion started. You also need to decide on your role in the discussion: will you be an active participant in the discussion? a facilitator? a devil's advocate if the discussion becomes too lopsided? In addition, decide if students must prepare for the discussion in advance and let them know what they need to do.

See appendix B for a sample discussion section lesson plan. See chapter 4 for more information about running a discussion.

Lecture Classes

In an information-intensive course, you may find yourself with a list of points that need to be explained to supplement the general lecture, and another lecture or a minilecture for part of the class may be the most efficient way to impart the information. Still encourage as much participation as possible; take advantage of the smaller size of a section and try to allow students to be more active in the learning process. Make a list on the board of points you will cover and have students help you flesh them out as you go through them. If possible, use more structured class plans like "Consolidating Lists" or "Information Exchange" (see chap. 6). However, if the course material on a given day requires you to lecture without much student participation, be sure to alert your students that you are departing from your usual format and briefly explain your reasons for doing so.

In today's day and age, many instructors are turning to PowerPoint for lectures. We know PowerPoint is "sexy," but we encourage you to consider the following pros and cons of using it.

PROS   PowerPoint provides a convenient way to store and present video clips, digital images, graphs, and charts.

It can save the instructor from having to write the lecture outline on the board or provide it on an overhead or handout.

CONS   PowerPoint moves too fast for students (or any human mind!). Either students are too busy copying slide content to process your lecture, or students, expecting the slides to be available after class, check out.

It restricts your ability to be spontaneous in the presentation of the material.

It can limit your ability to shape your lecture in response to students' questions and needs.
See appendix C for a sample lecture lesson plan.

Structured Student Activities

For highly structured, activity-based classes, you will want to make the following decisions before class begins and write them into your lesson plan.

- Will you divide students into groups and, if so, how?

- What instructions will the students need, and how will they get them?

- Will you be writing information on the board? (If so, write out what you will put on the board on your lesson plan so you can just copy it when you get to class.)

- How will you wrap up the lesson?
  See chapter 6 for specific lesson plans for structured student activities.

Time Management

It is fair to expect students to arrive to class on time, but in turn, you must respect their schedules and let them out on time.

Starting on Time

It is critical that you establish the practice of starting class on time. If you wait for the last few students to straggle in, it only encourages tardiness, and students will continue to come later and later. It also provides no incentive for typically punctual students to come on time. Once students realize that they will miss important material if they are late, most will come on time.

Keeping Time during Class

Prioritize class time. Decide what absolutely must get done that day and give yourself a time cushion, either at the end of an activity or at the end of class. You will probably want to have a watch or clock available, especially if there is no clock in the room or if it is behind you. You may want to put the watch or clock on the table or desk next to you so that you are not constantly looking at your wrist. You have the right to tell students not to start packing up their bags five minutes early, but in exchange, you must end class on time without this or another warning signal from them.

Organizing Space

Keep the physical limitations of your classroom in mind when you are crafting your lesson plans. For example, you will have trouble running an extended full-class discussion if the students' chairs are bolted to the floor in rows. If you feel too limited by the physical realities of your classroom (e.g., it is too small), do not hesitate to seek to be assigned to a more appropriate room.

Arranging Students

If possible, you should arrange the classroom before your students arrive. If not, have your students help you. It may seem like a hassle to have students pushing chairs around the room, and they may look at you like you're crazy when you tell them to do it, but it will make all the difference in how well a classroom discussion goes. Chair arrangement will depend on class format. In all cases, try to ensure that you can see every student's eyes.

Lecture Oriented

If you will be spending most of the time "imparting knowledge" to your wide-eyed students, every student should be able to see you and the board and have a place to write. This usually requires a more traditional students-facing-teacher classroom setup.

Discussion Oriented

If you are trying to encourage students to talk with each other about the material, no one should be looking at anyone else's back. A circle is usually the best arrangement—and make it a good circle. Students naturally create lackadaisical circles, with some students only half in and some students centered. Take the reins and force them to practice their geometric skills in creating a fairly round, well-balanced circle. Lop-sided circles almost invariably lead to poorly balanced discussions.

Lecture and Discussion Oriented

If you are starting with a lecture and then moving into a full-class discussion, wait until it is time for the discussion to ask students to arrange their desks or chairs in a circle. You then can use the movement of everyone into a circle as an obvious signal that full-class discussion is about to begin (and it's always a good way to make sure that everyone is awake!). Or you can put students in a semicircle for the entire class, such that they can see the board and talk with each other.

Placing Yourself

Again, where you put yourself in the classroom depends on the kind of teaching you are doing.

Lecture Oriented

Naturally this places you in the front of the classroom. You can lessen the distance between you and your students by moving tables, podiums, and so on, out of the way if they stand between you and the students. In order to keep your students awake and interested, you may want to move around the front of the classroom (a good reason to move large, sharp-cornered furniture) or even around the entire classroom.

Discussion Oriented

Once you have created a near-perfect circle, place yourself as part of that circle. You may want to keep yourself near the board if you will need to use it.

Lecture and Discussion Oriented

If you are doing a combination of lecture and discussion, you may want to arrange the chairs in a half circle with you in the front. When you are lecturing, you should stand, especially if you need to use the board. When you join the class in discussion, you should sit (behind a front table, at a chair, on the table, etc.). Remember that how you place yourself, whether you stand or sit, affects how students will interact with you and the material that you are presenting at that moment.

Interacting with the Professor

If you are leading a discussion section for a larger lecture course, your relationship with the professor can be easy, treacherously tricky, or anywhere in between. The professor may or may not explicitly set guidelines for your section—both situations can be problematic or productive. There are some basic guidelines that both you and the professor should follow.

Feedback to the Professor

Because of your close interaction with the students and their work, you have access to information about the course and the students that the professor may not. It is your responsibility to tell the professor certain information about students. A basic list:

- a concept the professor covered in lecture that confused students and requires review;

- a section of an exam on which many students did poorly;

- consistent problems students are having with writing assignments or their writing;

- a student who is causing problems in section or who is consistently not coming to section;

- a student who is consistently complaining about grades.

Feedback from the Professor

The amount of help and guidance that professors offer to their teaching assistants varies, but there are many ways that professors can make your life easier if they are willing. You should not hesitate to ask for any of the following, even if they are not offered:

- an outline or other guidance on information the professor would like covered in section;

- clarification of attendance or late work policies;

- a meeting with you about what material will be covered on the exam;

- a meeting to go over an exam, its answers, and a grading policy;

- a few graded papers for the first assignment so that you can get a sense of the professor's expectations and grading range.

Your Public Relationship with the Professor

No matter what your personal feelings about the professor and their teaching style, you must keep your public relationship with them professional and maintain a "united front." You should not criticize the professor in front of your students, even if they are complaining, and you should not question the professor's abilities as a scholar or a teacher. You may use section as a time to present alternate viewpoints or additional information, but you also are responsible for helping the students understand the material the professor presents in class, so you may not dismiss it.

After a lecture with which you do not agree:

DON'T "Don't pay attention to what Professor Engels was saying in class yesterday. He is a Marxist, and he still believes in that outdated theory; he doesn't seem interested in recent scholarship, so I'll have to fill you in."

DO "There are many schools of thought and interpretation when it comes to a question like this one. Professor Engels is presenting a Marxist position. Let's make sure that you understand the elements involved in this interpretation and its strengths and weaknesses. Then if you're interested, I can explain some of the alternative interpretations."

After a student complains to you about the professor:

DON'T "I understand what you're saying. Professor Leslie can be dismissive and isn't always good about answering questions. Other students have had trouble in the past. And she isn't very good about answering my questions either."

DO "I know that Professor Leslie can be intimidating sometimes, but she is very knowledgeable, and you should feel free to go to her office hours with questions. You are also always welcome to talk to me about material you don't understand—we both are here as resources for you."

Remember that some day soon you too may be a professor teaching a course with teaching assistants; think about how you would want these graduate students to treat you and the material that you present in lecture and act accordingly.

Addressing Problems

Every class comes with its own unique challenges. Having difficulties with a class, or in your dealings with an individual student, is a normal and expectable part of teaching. Here, and throughout the remainder of this book, you'll find guidance on addressing some of the most common problems that college teachers face. In general, we encourage you to insert an important step between recognizing and responding to problems. We call this step "diagnosing the problem" and have found that taking the time to understand the root cause of a problem goes a long way toward fixing it.

Making a Diagnosis

Once you have identified a problem in your class, you'll want to investigate its cause before deciding upon a solution.

EXAMPLE   One student arrives to class late every day.

DON'T   Develop an ad hoc lateness policy; lock the classroom door once class begins; humiliate the student in front of their peers.

DO   Find time to catch the student after class and ask why they are coming to class late.

Using a Diagnosis to Find a Solution

Once you understand the reasons behind a particular problem, you and the student(s) will be able to come up with the most appropriate solution.

EXAMPLES   The student is consistently late because the class that they have before yours is on the far side of campus, making a timely arrival to your class impossible. You and the student can discuss ways to diminish the disruption of the student's late arrival.

The student complains that the class is too early. You remind the student that they knew the class time when they enrolled and that the lateness policy applies to early birds and night owls alike.

It is often the case that taking the time to diagnose the problem fixes the problem. For example, few students will continue to come to class late once an instructor has inquired about their lateness.

Further Reading

Bain, K. 2004. *What the Best College Teachers Do.* Cambridge: Harvard University Press.

Bligh, D. A. 2000. *What's the Use of Lectures?* San Francisco: Jossey-Bass.

Cannon, R., and D. Newble. 2000. *A Handbook for Teachers in Universities and Colleges: A Guide to Improving Teaching Methods.* 4th ed. London: Kogan Page.

Davis, B. G. 1993. *Tools for Teaching.* San Francisco: Jossey-Bass.

Fink, L. D. 2003. *Creating Significant Learning Experiences: An Integrated Approach to Designing College Courses.* San Francisco: Jossey-Bass.

Leamnson, R. 1999. *Thinking about Teaching and Learning: Developing Habits of Learning with First Year College and University Students.* Sterling, VA: Stylus; Oakhill, Eng.: Trentham Books.

Lowman, J. 1995. *Mastering the Techniques of Teaching.* 2d ed. San Francisco: Jossey-Bass.

McKeachie, W. J., and M. Svinicki. 2006. *McKeachie's Teaching Tips: Strategies, Research and Theory for College and University Teachers.* 12th ed. Boston: Houghton Mifflin.

Meagher, L. D., and T. G. Devine. 1993. *Handbook on College Teaching.* Durango, CO: Hollowbrook.

Tufte, E. R. 2003. *The Cognitive Style of PowerPoint.* Cheshire: Graphics Press.

Chapter 4
Running a Discussion

Running a good discussion is like writing a good essay: you need a strong opening, a well-organized body, and a coherent ending. Most of this chapter is relevant only to teaching assistants leading discussion sections or teaching introductory (probably nonscience) courses. However, these tips will be helpful to anyone running a discussion-oriented class.

Discussions versus Task-Based Participation

Just because sections are often called "discussion sections" does not mean that all the student participation in your classroom will be actual "discussion." (It seems more obvious that at universities that call sections "recitation sections," neither you nor the students are spending the whole time reciting.) It is useful to distinguish between two different kinds of student participation: genuine discussion and task-based participation. Both can be very productive learning experiences, and the decision about which to use will depend on your goals for any given class.

In a genuine discussion, you begin with real questions to which you do not have a definitive answer, and you are open to and interested in your students' responses. You do not have an agenda about exactly what material needs to be covered and how. In other words, your goal for the discussion focuses on having the students think with you about an issue rather than covering predetermined content in a particular sequence.

Sometimes you do have an agenda for what specific material needs to be covered, and you want students to participate in the process of covering that material. Obviously, this is not a "genuine discussion" because you know where you are headed—and your students know you have a destination in mind. But it can be a better learning experience for students to participate rather than simply listen to you lecture. The deadliest "discussions" happen when an instructor frames what is a task-based activity as real, open discussion.

As you prepare your lesson plan, you want to be clear with yourself about whether your class will be a discussion or task-based participation (or both). You will then be able to be clear with your students about what you have planned and why.

Arranging the Classroom

The physical arrangement of the classroom will influence the quality of your discussion. Students who are sitting where they cannot be seen by you or their classmates may not feel expected or encouraged to participate in the discussion. We recommend that you help your students to create a well-formed circle.

See chapter 3, "Organizing Space," for more information on organizing classroom space.

Initiating Student Participation

Use your discussion opening to inform students of the topic you have in mind for class and of your expectations for the day's activities. Remember, you already have spent a great deal of time planning the class; students, however, arrive with no idea of what you have in mind. Your opening orients your students to how your class plan fits within the broader goals of the course. Several ways to introduce your topic and generate student participation are detailed here.

Make a List

You can ask a question to the class and generate a list of responses on the board, or you can ask each student to share one idea or item off the top of their head. (If you are not using the board for such an activity, jot down notes to yourself on a piece of paper as students talk.) You then have material with which to begin.

EXAMPLES   *Discussion:* "Let's make two lists here on the board of all the pros and cons you can think of for the use of politically correct language."

Task-based participation: "The author of the article uses at least four different kinds of evidence to support her argument. When you write your papers, you will also be drawing on these kinds of evidence. So take five minutes in

pairs to identify all the different kinds of evidence you can,
and then we'll go over them together."

Freewriting

Freewriting can help students to formulate their ideas before participating in a full-class activity. Have all the students get out a piece of paper;
give them a question and five or ten minutes to answer it. Tell them you
will not be collecting the paper; you just want to see their pens moving
the full five or ten minutes. Once they have done this, every student has
something to say, and you can move into your activity from there. After
the time for freewriting has ended, you can call on students—or ask students to volunteer—to read part of what they have written.

EXAMPLES　　*Discussion:* "Take out a piece of paper—I'm going to ask
you to write continuously for six minutes. On Monday in
lecture we watched a documentary about endangered
species in Alaska. Take this time to write about your reactions to the film, whatever they were: questions you had,
emotions you felt, whatever comes to mind."

Task-based participation: "Get out a piece of paper—you
are not going to have to turn this in. Take the next five
minutes and write down as much as you can remember
from yesterday's explanation in lecture of DNA coding.
Then we can work together on filling in any holes."

Pair and Share

This tried-and-true teaching strategy is a terrific way to get students
talking to each other and then moving into a full-class activity. Put students into pairs and give each pair a task or question. Depending on
your lesson plan, you may want to give different tasks to each pair or
have them all work on the same question. Make the goal clear: for
example, as a pair they will tell their classmates about their thoughts on
a particular issue; they will share two ideas with the class; they should
write a paragraph that they then will give to another pair, and so forth.
Pair time allows shyer students to check out their ideas with one other
person before sharing them with the group, and it gives all the students
a very informal "warm-up" time before a fuller class discussion.

EXAMPLES   *Discussion:* "Find a partner. Together, make a decision about which two diagnoses might be removed or dramatically changed in the next edition of the psychiatric diagnostic manual. Be sure to have a justification for your choices."

Task-based participation: "Choose a partner and together take five minutes to come up with four examples of 'abnormal' behavior that are situationally dependent. At the end of five minutes, I will go around the room and ask you to share your responses with the rest of the class."

Small Group Activities

Small group activities follow the same format as Pair and Share; give groups a question or task and make the goal clear. Then, have each group integrate their work into a full-class activity. Figure out ahead of time how you are going to make the groups. You can form groups by where students are sitting, which allows friends to talk comfortably with friends but which can also (a) lead to some discussion unrelated to the course and (b) prevent students from meeting other students in the class. You can "number off" around the room and have all the "ones" work together, and so on. You can make groups ahead of time if you want to ensure that you have at least one good talker in each group.

See chapter 6, "Debate: Grouping Strategies," for more information on putting students into working groups.

Read a Passage from the Text

If you want to talk about a text in class, you can "warm up" by reading and discussing one passage from the text. Reasons to use this strategy:

- It gives students a foothold for discussing the entire text.

- It reminds students what the text is about (remember: students may well have done work for other classes since the time they read this text).

- If some students have not read the entire text, it still engages them in the planned activity for the day.

Pick a passage that highlights whatever theme(s) you want to address first and ask a student to read it aloud. Then, have a series of follow-up questions prepared. If you are trying to encourage students to do close reading, use this as an opportunity to dive into the details of the passage.

See appendix D for an annotated passage with several possible follow-up questions.

Encouraging Active Student Reading

You should give your students tips about how they can prepare readings before they come to class. Specifically, college students should be urged to start reading with a pen or pencil in hand. Help your students see the utility of marking noteworthy passages as they read. The most effective way to do this is to have them mark up passages during class so that they get used to the idea of writing in their books and see how this can help them do close readings.

EXAMPLE   *Task-based participation:* Have students mark all the passive constructions in a lab write-up and then talk about how use of passive constructions affects the tone of the writing.

You also can give students this type of assignment ahead of time, so that they have something to look for while they do the reading.

EXAMPLE   *Discussion:* "As you're reading, mark all the passages where you think the material is extraneous—in other words, you don't see why it's there. Then together we'll be able to see if you all agree and talk about why the author may have included this material in the novel."

Ask a Question

The right question to the full class (which is, of course, sitting in a perfect circle) can get a good discussion rolling. See the following for tips on quality questioning.

See chapter 6 for specific structured class plans that end with a discussion.

Effective Discussion Questions

Genuine discussions require effective questions. Asking good discussion questions is a skill that takes experience and preparation. You cannot walk into class and generate a meaningful discussion by asking questions off the top of your head. Instructors who begin by asking, "So what did you think of the reading?" are almost always greeted with painful silence. Students respond well to questions that are specific and interesting, questions that invite original contributions. Students do not respond well to broad, basic, or "fake" questions. In general, focus on asking "how" and "why" questions rather than "what" and "who" questions.

Asking the First Questions

Write out a series of discussion questions as you prepare the lesson plans for the class. These questions should be directly related to your goal(s) for that class. They should be questions that interest you and will interest your students. Be prepared to think up more questions as you go, but it is a nice safety net to have a few written questions beforehand. Also be prepared to play devil's advocate, to challenge students' views if no one else will.

You may choose to start with a big question that will (you hope!) generate sustained discussion. You may also choose to start with smaller, more discrete questions that can build toward a more substantial question connected to your goal(s) for the class.

Overbroad Questions

Don't "What did you think of the reading?"

Do "If you were a dialect speaker from Tennessee, how do you think you would feel about the author's description of your dialect?"

"Talking down" Questions

Don't "Who is the author?"

Do "Could you tell anything about the author's background from the article?" (Be prepared to tell them about the author if you are going to ask a question like this.)

"Read my Mind" Questions

Don't   "Why is human cloning unethical?"

Do   "Imagine you sit on this university's ethics panel, and a professor wants to start a human cloning program. What questions would you want to have answered and why?"

Questions with Right and Wrong Answers

Don't   "What is the author's point in this essay?"

Do   "Let's read the first paragraph together. . . . Did it make you want to keep reading? Why or why not?"

"Testing for Reading" Questions

Don't   "What three facts does the author use to support her contention that teaching assistants should be worshiped?"

Do   (If necessary) "How many of you finished the reading for today? What happened? What are we going to do about this?"

You will notice that some of the "Don't" examples for discussion questions could legitimately introduce a task-based activity. It helps students when you do not confuse discussions and task-based participation.

Why Students May Not Talk

At times, you may ask the most compelling questions imaginable and still be met with cold silence from your students. Here are a few causes of and solutions to the silent-student syndrome.

Peer Pressure

Peer pressure is at work in every classroom, and students usually are as (or more) concerned with what their peers think of them as they are with what you think of them. They do not want to say something stupid, and they do not want to look like a teacher's pet. So you will do better asking questions that solicit opinions rather than right/wrong answers because students run less risk of "losing face" with these kinds of answers.

Time to Think

One of the most painful parts of starting a discussion can be the silence. Get used to it. You thought up the question before class, but the students are hearing it for the first time, and they need a minute or two to think about it. Let the silence hang there for longer than you think you can bear (make yourself count to twenty slowly); generally a student will finally step in to fill the void and start the discussion. If you know that you are asking a tough question, tell the class that you will give them some time to think before soliciting answers. This way, the silence is planned rather than awkward.

Very Difficult Material

Even when students are prepared for class, they may not participate if they feel overwhelmed by the difficulty of the material. Sharing with them that you find parts of the material difficult can authorize them to speak about the material as well. It does not diminish your authority to acknowledge that material is difficult. You can say something like: "This a very challenging reading. I know that I am feeling confused by the first paragraph on p. 12. Why don't we start here—I am hoping some of you have insights about what this means. Then we can look at places where you felt stumped."

Lack of Preparation

If no student steps up to break the silence and you cannot bear it any longer, do not ask an easier question: "Okay, who is the author?" Why should any student stoop to answer this question? If you are trying to determine whether or not students did the reading, ask them. They will be surprisingly (often brutally) honest with you.

Class Dynamics

Depending on the makeup of the class, you may find that some students do not feel comfortable volunteering to participate. You need to be particularly aware of the willingness of female students and students in some way representing a minority voice in the classroom to take part in full-class discussions. Be conscious of how often you call on and in other ways involve students of different genders, races, and ages and work to facilitate the participation of the students who seem more reticent to volunteer their opinions in this setting.

Quiet Students

Some very eager and interested students do not feel comfortable participating in full-class discussions. Be sympathetic and be careful about putting these students on the spot.

See "Handling Discussion-Stopping Students: Quiet Students" in this chapter for more information on how to handle quiet students.

Outside Forces

There are times during the term (e.g., midterms, fraternity and sorority rush) when students tend to be tired or stressed or overly busy or distracted. They drag themselves to class, but their presence is merely physical. If you try to start a discussion on one of these days and you find that you are facing exhaustion-induced silence, try stepping back and asking the students directly, and empathetically, what is going on (an activity we call "meta-teaching"). They will appreciate your recognition that they have concerns outside your class. And more importantly, it will start students talking. You then can guide the conversation toward the lesson you have planned.

See chapter 9, "Meta-teaching," for more details on talking to your students about the class.

Facilitating Discussion

One of the most important elements of a successful classroom discussion is a good balance of voices, including your own.

Your Role as the Teacher

Navigating your role in a full-class discussion is one of the most difficult parts of learning to teach. Do not become frustrated with yourself if you are feeling less than stellar in this area; it can and will take years to get comfortable as a discussion leader.

The crucial element is to think of yourself as a facilitator: you are helping the students talk about a particular topic, and what they say may or may not surprise you. Be prepared to let the discussion follow its natural course as long as it is not moving too far away from your goals for the class. As long as the discussion is germane to the topic, it is most important that students are talking about issues that *they* find intriguing. You do not have to know all the answers along the way, and you should feel free to look to them for their expertise. You will find that they often will be able to answer each other's questions; and they can find it empowering to be able to do so.

As a discussion facilitator, you should keep in mind some overarching goals.

Help students participate.

Don't   Embarrass a student for any comment. You never want a student to be sorry they spoke.

Do   Take all comments seriously and help students find what is most important, interesting, or accurate in what they are saying.

Regularly provide positive feedback to students for their contributions (e.g., "Great question" or "You know, I never thought about that before").

Encourage equal participation by students of different genders, races, and ages.

Help students speak and respond to each other.

Don't   Respond to every student comment yourself. Students may then speak only to you, and discussions may become stilted as students wait for your intervention after each comment.

Do   Encourage student responses: "How do the rest of you feel about Harriet's comment that no one version of a country's history is better than another?"

Encourage students to respond to each other directly (without raising hands, if possible). Step in to summarize or redirect the discussion when necessary.

Help students explore a variety of viewpoints.

Don't   Weigh in with your own opinion too quickly. Students are often looking for "canned" or simple answers to difficult questions, and they may adopt your opinion as "truth."

Do   Solicit a variety of opinions; ask students to come up with counterpoints to their own and each other's arguments.

Help keep discussion moving.

Don't   Let the discussion get stuck because an interesting topic has been exhausted.

Do   Summarize the content of the discussion when it is beginning to wind down. Help students consider a fresh but related topic.

Help keep the discussion on track.

Don't   Let students stray too far from your goals for the class.

Do   Step in when you sense a serious detour. Explain that while this is an interesting line of thought, it will take you too far afield.

Help students see gaps in their understanding.

Don't   Tell students that they are wrong or that they missed the point.

Do   Acknowledge that this is a confusing issue or problem, gently correct the misunderstanding or error, and point out where the student is on the right track.

Help students see connections and the bigger picture.

Don't   Let the discussion jump freely from topic to topic.

Do   Tie together various students' comments on one topic, explicitly stating connections (e.g., "Karen, your question brings us back to Jared's earlier comment").

      Summarize points and counterpoints or dilemmas with which students are struggling. Taking notes on students' comments as the discussion progresses will help you here.

Handling Sensitive Material

At times, your course may call for the discussion of a sensitive topic. Questions involving issues of gender, race, culture, class, sexual orientation, or any other "political" topic will make the task of running a free-flowing, balanced, and thoughtful discussion more challenging than usual.

Lay Some Ground Rules

Acknowledge from the outset that you are discussing a sensitive topic. Make it clear to your students that you expect them to treat each other with respect. Encourage them to be respectful of each other's opinions and to question the quality of the arguments offered, not the validity of each other's personal beliefs.

EXAMPLE "Over the weekend you read about the debate over affirmative action. I suspect that this is an area where many of you have strong personal feelings. The fact that this is a sensitive topic makes it all the more important that we are able to discuss it in a forum like this. We want to explore all sides of this issue, so don't feel that the points you raise have to match your personal beliefs. By the same token, we must remember that we are evaluating arguments, not the people who raise them. This is going to be a very challenging issue to discuss, but I think that we can do it well. I know that you all can deal with this topic and each other in a sensitive way."

Create a Safe Space

Ask your students to listen to each other and not to judge anyone else too quickly. If they disagree, they should speak up to try to show their classmate(s) where they think they are wrong. Stewing in silent indignation is not fair and does not help others learn.

Tell Students to Beware of "Us" and "Them"

Remind your students they cannot tell much by looking at each other. In many cases, they will not know if one of their classmates is HIV positive, a member of a racial or religious minority, a communist, a welfare recipient, or anything else unless that classmate chooses to volunteer the information. Students should discuss the topic at hand with these possibilities in mind.

Question Carefully

You can encourage students to think about material in a thoughtful (as opposed to reactive) way by directing their thinking with your questions. It often helps to start the discussion in an "objective" way, asking about what arguments exist on either side of an issue or what relevant ideas students have heard. In this way, you are not directly soliciting students' personal opinions, thus creating a safer space.

EXAMPLE   "What political influences tend to bring about welfare reforms? What ulterior motives for these reforms exist on both sides of the congressional aisle?"
See chapter 6, "Debate" and "Pros and Cons," for specific class plans that work well for handling sensitive or controversial issues.

Be the Devil's Advocate

Discussions of sensitive material can become lopsided for any number of reasons. Students may be hesitant to say anything that does not sound politically correct, a variety of views may not be present in the classroom, or students may feel reluctant to challenge each other's thinking. If the discussion is not well rounded, you need to offer the underrepresented position, regardless of your personal feelings on the matter.

EXAMPLE   "But one could argue (and people do) that people on welfare don't want to work. What evidence possibly supports this argument?"

Handling Discussion-Stopping Students

At times, students will behave in a way that can potentially stifle even the most promising discussion. This can happen because the students are misbehaving or not doing anything at all. Never allow yourself to become visibly angry with them or with the entire class. Expressing anger with students is a no-win situation for you. It displays a loss of control and professional demeanor, which is more likely to exacerbate the students' behavior than improve it. Instead, try these techniques.

Quiet Students

In every class, there will be quieter students who do not feel as (or at all) comfortable participating in a full-class discussion. One of the benefits of the Pair and Share activity or small group activities is that they provide these students with more of a voice. Once you have identified who these students are, you should think carefully about when you want to call on them in class. Make eye contact with them during a discussion to see if they might want to voice an opinion.

DON'T   Put quiet students on the spot by calling on them in a full-class discussion—it will only make speaking in class more frightening.

DO   Call on quiet students after a freewriting exercise when you know that they have something already prepared or after they have been discussing an issue in a pair.

Do not hesitate to say something to these quieter students in a one-on-one setting. If one of these students spoke up in class, you can reinforce their participation by writing about it in an e-mail or in your comments on a returned paper.

EXAMPLE   "Thanks for making your classmates reconsider their opinions by asking about the consequences of banning cigarettes. I hope we'll continue to hear your voice in class—you have lots of good things to contribute."

You also can remind students in a midterm conference that participation is part of their final grade and that if they do not feel comfortable talking in a full-class setting, you need to see them making a real effort in small groups or talking to you on e-mail or during office hours. There are many ways to participate.

Disruptive Students

Disruptive students are not necessarily loud and obnoxious. Rather, they are students who choose, often in subtle ways, not to participate in the class or who encourage other students not to participate. They are often the students who look or act like they do not want to be in your class.

Do not teach to disruptive students. They are the squeaky wheels, and you will often find yourself bending over backward to please them or get them interested in class.

DON'T   Screw up a good discussion by trying to force a recalcitrant student to participate.

Do   Keep your radar focused on all the students and recognize that there may be some students who are not going to immerse themselves in the classroom activities.

The other students are aware of the disruptive students' behavior, and they too are often happy to let these nonparticipants sit on the sidelines. Here are some disruptive student Hall of Famers and some suggestions for what you can do.

The Newspaper Reader

Class is rolling, and a student is still reading the newspaper. The most effective remedy to this situation is the direct approach: "Joe, this is not the time to read the paper. You can do that after class." It does not hurt to show students that you do not tolerate blatant displays of inattention, and very few students will continue to read a newspaper after being directly told not to do so.

The Whisperers

You are talking to the class or a student is speaking, and there are two students whispering to each other about clearly non-class-related things. You can try the direct approach of asking them to stop talking when others are talking (you can interrupt your own monologue or wait until the other student is finished speaking). You might say something like "When you guys are talking it makes it hard for the rest of us to hear each other; please save it for after class." You also can walk over to stand near them if you are lecturing (and you are a roving lecturer). Or you can halt the discussion and wait until they notice that their whispers are the only noise in the room. At times, students do whisper to each other about class-related ideas. You can feel free to give students the benefit of the doubt and (kindly) ask them to share their thoughts with the class. This approach engages interested students and stops non-class chitchat.

The Discussion Hog

Every time you ask a question or ask for a volunteer, this student's hand shoots up or they just begin talking. Very often these students have the best intentions and are friendly, outgoing people; but they are still unfairly monopolizing full-class discussion and your attention. A direct and gentle approach usually works well with these students.

EXAMPLE   "Sylvia, I'll come back to you shortly; let's see if someone else wants to grab the floor for a minute."

If the student persists in monopolizing class time after a few class meetings where you have tried to manage their behavior during class, arrange to meet with the student individually. Reinforce for them that you appreciate their participation in the class but remind them of their responsibility to let others speak.

The Antagonistic Debater

This student verbally challenges you or other students on a regular basis. Perhaps they feel that you are too liberal or too conservative in your views, or perhaps they simply enjoy disagreeing with you to see if you'll get flustered. You must put up with a healthy amount of disagreement in the classroom. You want to encourage students to question their classmates' and their teachers' statements as they would any others. But you also have the right to expect these challenging remarks to be phrased appropriately. When the student verbalizes a contradictory opinion, feel free to ask follow-up questions and force them to articulate their ideas. And be sure to answer antagonistic remarks with thoughtful consideration; in this way, you move the discussion out of empty rhetoric and back into intellectual discourse.

EXAMPLES   "Why is Darwin's theory of evolution 'stupid'? (Is 'stupid' really the best description, Irene?) What problems does it present, and what do you see as the alternatives?"

"Joe, you say that you think this article is ridiculously biased. How do you think the author could strengthen her argument?"

The Bomb Dropper

Occasionally, you will come across students who use explosive language to express their ideas. Few teachers forget the first time a student makes a comment so offensive that the entire class comes to a halt. Managing this classroom event is a challenge for even the most seasoned instructor. Once you get your jaw off the floor you must do your best to turn the student's comment into a teachable moment.

EXAMPLES   "Steven has proposed that women who are raped want sex but are afraid to ask for it. The tension created by his comment is palpable. Why does his statement cause such an emotional response? Can we pause for a moment and think through how his idea could be engaged in an academic, not a polemical, manner?"

"Mary suggests that white people should be allowed to use the 'n-word' freely given that many African Americans now do so. Would the feeling in the room be different right now if Mary had not elected to use the actual word in making her comment? Why? Mary's idea is an interesting one; can someone raise the same question in a way that gets a fruitful discussion going?"

The Silent Glarer

Every class meeting, no matter what you are doing or saying, this student is sitting in their chair, arms folded, glaring at you to let you know that they are not going to participate in—let alone enjoy—your class under any circumstances. At times, this student may take a break from their glaring to mutter obviously derogatory comments about you and/or the class to their neighbor. For the first one or two class meetings, try to involve this student as best you can while being fair to the other students: call on them as you would a quiet student or try to put them in a talkative small group. If these efforts don't succeed, you must waste no time in reaching out to this student. Do not give in to the temptation to ignore the student's silent protest. Their attitude is deadly to class morale, and their immature behavior can often be addressed effectively with a mature response.

Catch the student after class or drop them an e-mail to let them know that you are aware that the course is not working well for them and to invite them to identify their concerns. With substantive feedback, you will have a basis for working with the student to solve the problem. Even if the student ignores your overture, most silent glarers will be better behaved in class once they've been approached directly.

EXAMPLE   "Jonas, I'm sensing that you have some concerns about the class. It would be useful for me to know what they are to see if there's anything we can do."

> "After teaching a class in which I had ignored a silent glarer for the entire semester, I happened to be enrolled in a class where one of the other students alternated between silent glaring and quiet complaining about the (very competent) instructor! As a fellow student, I was incredibly distracted by 'who's-with-me-in-thinking-this-teacher-sucks?' dynamic created by the student. I was desperate for the instructor to intervene. It made me realize that I should have said something to my own silent glarer."

Wrapping up Discussion

Think of a class as a well-written essay or article. The last paragraph(s) should remind the reader of the question they are to consider or the point they are to remember. It may sound rehearsed to think of your closing statements ahead of time, but the best instructors have as solid an ending as a beginning to their lectures or discussions. If you start the class with a list or story, perhaps you want to return to that. If you start with a passage from the text, perhaps you want to return to that or another passage from the text to finish. You can always return to your goals for the class and remind students why you all did what you did.

Do not end class purely by time.

DON'T   "Oh my gosh, I guess that's the end of our time. We'll finish up this discussion at the beginning of the next class. Think about what we've discussed!"

DO   Leave yourself enough time to summarize what was discussed, to tie things up, and to provide students with a sense of what they have accomplished that day.

Do not feel you have to give the answer.

DON'T   "The price we have paid for technological advances is too
high. My research focuses on what we've done to the environment, and we cannot possibly justify it."

Do   "You've all expressed some very contradictory opinions that
show how difficult the question is. There are valid arguments
on both sides, and smart people disagree on this issue. The
fundamental problem is that it comes down to how we feel
about the importance of technology and what we're willing to
sacrifice for progress on this front. Next week, we'll be talking
about water pollution, which will raise many of the same
issues, so keep this discussion in mind while you're doing the
reading this week."

Try to relate this class to those before and after it, as well as to the
course goals.

Students benefit if they can understand the progression of the course,
how last week's discussion relates to this week's debate. In your role as
class guide, help students see the progression of the course. They will be
better able to engage and discuss specific course material when they
know how the material fits into the broader context of the course.

EXAMPLES   "Today we have been talking about whether an anthropol-
ogist can ever claim to understand another culture. Is
observation sufficient for understanding? When you read
the article for this week, keep this question in mind as you
read about John Gaze's methodology. Does he have
sufficient evidence to make his claims? We'll start with this
issue next time."

"Last week you all raised the question of whether Shake-
speare's poetry was ever written to be read or only to be
heard and how that might change the way in which we
analyze the sonnets. Today we've been looking at poems
clearly meant to be read, poems that lose perhaps their
essence if we only hear them. This theme of the oral versus
the written nature of poetry is something that we will
return to often as we trace a history of poetry."

Provide positive feedback about what went well in class.

EXAMPLE   "This is an incredibly complex problem set, and at the beginning of class, I said that this would be a difficult review for us to pull off successfully. I am impressed with the way you all stepped up to the challenge."

Although it sounds like an easy thing to do, bringing a class to a meaningful conclusion is an acquired skill. When you first start teaching, your efforts to bring the class to closure may feel awkward; as you gain experience, you will be able to integrate your conclusion more and more naturally into the flow of the class.

Further Reading

Brookfield, S. D. 1990. *The Skillful Teacher: On Technique, Trust, and Responsiveness in the Classroom.* San Francisco: Jossey-Bass.

Davis, B. G. 1993. *Tools for Teaching.* San Francisco: Jossey-Bass.

Filene, P. 2005. *The Joy of Teaching: A Practical Guide for New College Instructors.* Chapel Hill: University of North Carolina Press.

Lowman, J. 1995. *Mastering the Techniques of Teaching.* 2d ed. San Francisco: Jossey-Bass.

McKeachie, W. J., and M. Svinicki. 2006. *McKeachie's Teaching Tips: Strategies, Research, and Theory for College and University Teachers.* 12th ed. Boston: Houghton Mifflin.

Richner, S., and L. Weir, eds. 1995. *Beyond Political Correctness: Toward the Inclusive University.* Toronto: University of Toronto Press.

Chapter 5
Problem Sets and Laboratories

Much teaching in mathematics, the natural sciences, and foreign languages involves a "hands-on" approach. In other fields, classes in methodology, data collection, and statistics have incorporated a similar kind of learning. Teaching in these fields differs, in some significant ways, from much of the teaching in the humanities and social sciences. This chapter is designed to address issues specific to teaching assistants who teach from problem sets or exercises or who run laboratories.

Teaching with Problem Sets

Most mathematics courses and many courses in the hard sciences require students to complete problem sets on a regular basis. All courses in foreign languages require students to complete practice exercises. For the teaching assistant, this means that much of the section or the course itself will involve reviewing or otherwise incorporating these homework assignments. The key is to find ways to make this activity productive and participatory—an active learning experience for the students. In the remainder of this section, the term *problem set* is used to apply to any assignment of questions students are expected to answer.

The Function of Problem Sets

Problem sets are important and useful as a tool through which students acquire skills and demonstrate an understanding of larger concepts. Your teaching of problem sets should reinforce this relationship between problem sets (the "hands-on part") and the material of the course (the "abstract part"). Your job is not over when students have all the correct answers to a problem set in hand; they must also understand the concept behind the answers and how this concept could be applied to other problems.

Setting Ground Rules at the Beginning of the Semester

Many students walk into math, science, and language classes expecting the focus to be on right and wrong answers. Instructors reinforce this expectation when their sole aim is to provide correct answers. Although accuracy is, of course, critical to math, science, and language learning, you need to stress for yourself and for your students the importance of good problem solving over perfect solutions. In the educational process, the key is often the journey, not the destination; students need to be able to chart their way through new problems in the future without your assistance.

From the beginning of the semester, make it clear to your students that you are an instructor who believes in the importance of persistence and risk taking as much as correct answers. For students to take this statement seriously, you need to structure the course so that it emphasizes the problem solving process.

In lower-level courses, students will often come in with vastly different backgrounds, particularly in math. You will undoubtedly encounter "math anxiety" in at least a few students; you may find this kind of anxiety to be more common with female students entering the sciences, which have historically been male-dominated disciplines. You may overhear students explaining their dislike or lack of success with comments such as "I'm just bad at math." It is important for you to remember that the same problem set can be simple for some students and almost impossible for others, and that competent students may feel doubtful of their abilities.

At the beginning of the semester, gauge the range of abilities and experience in the class. Emphasize to all students that *everyone* has to put in time and hard work to succeed in these fields and make yourself available to provide support for those students who need it (and who are willing to work for it). However, you cannot emphasize enough that it is up to the students to learn the material; you cannot do it for them.

Preliminaries for Lesson Plans

When you think about how to present material in math, science, and language classes, be creative in your approach. The traditional, linear approach to teaching this kind of material is often not the most effective. Students will see the material in this form in the book; you do not want to present it to them in the same form in class. You will need to decide how much time to spend lecturing, reviewing problem sets, and answering questions.

Writing Creative Lectures

Employ different strategies that will help illuminate the concept you want to cover. You can use visual aids (pictures, charts, graphs), verbal descriptions (story problems, real life applications), or physical props (tennis balls, Lincoln logs, pulleys and levers).

EXAMPLE   To teach the concept of pipelining in computer science, send pieces of paper down a row of students with each student drawing their own shape and passing on the paper each time you snap your fingers. They will then see the simultaneous functioning of the many parts of a multiple task.

With difficult concepts, use building blocks. Start with a simpler explanation or example of a concept and make sure that everyone understands. Then substitute gradually more difficult material into the example.

EXAMPLE   Set up a story of a farmer with a certain amount of fence with which he wants to enclose the largest possible area. Review how students might try to calculate this area. Then begin to substitute calculus symbols for the entities in this "real life" equation.

Metaphors and analogies can also helpfully explain complex and/or abstract concepts.

EXAMPLE   "This mathematical relationship can be paralleled to the codependence of foxes and bunnies. A certain number of foxes eat a certain number of bunnies to survive. Now, what happens to the bunnies if the fox population suddenly grows larger?"

Ways to Review Problem Sets

There are probably as many different variations on ways to review problem sets as there are different kinds of problem sets. Here are a few general types of reviews with sample lesson plans and guidelines.

Teaching-Assistant-Led Review

At times, it may be most efficient and effective for the teaching assistant to lead the problem set review. Encourage as much student participation in this process as possible.

Steps for the Review

1. Start by establishing the goals for the review: for example, how many problems you expect to cover and how thoroughly; how students should be involved in the review process.

2. Begin with a problem of your choosing or ask students to decide which problem they would like to cover first.

3. If a student chooses the problem, ask them where they got stuck and then determine how many other students got stuck at this same level. If you have chosen the problem, poll the class on where they ran into difficulties.

4. Once you have determined the area(s) of difficulty, respond with questions to the class (not just to the student asking the question) about how to begin working on a solution. You may want to ask them to choose among several options about how to proceed; if you offer only one suggestion, most students will agree to it, whether it is the most helpful option or not.

   EXAMPLES   "Do you want to draw a picture?"

   "Do you want to work backward from the answer?"

   "Do you want to solve a simpler problem first?"

   "Do you want to substitute easier numbers for harder ones in the equation?"

5. If one student in the class has figured out how to do the problem and volunteers this information, you can ask them to explain the solution to their classmates if they are comfortable doing so.

   See "Student Presentations" in this chapter for more information on spontaneous student teaching.

6. As you continue to review more problems, you may find that you want to be more thorough in your responses to the first few questions and then provide more summary or specific help with later questions.

7. End the review by telling students how you expect them to follow up on this material: for example, correct the problem set and turn it in next class; take five minutes and write down lingering questions so you can know where there is still confusion; try the next few (perhaps harder) problems in the book to see if they can apply their new understanding.

Guidelines for the Review

- Use questions from students to focus your teaching efforts. They are showing you what they do not understand and where they need your assistance.

- Never humiliate students who ask questions, however simple. They (and their classmates) will only be reluctant to ask again if they feel singled out for having revealed their confusion or lack of understanding.

- Be conscious of how much and how often different students are talking and encourage equal participation by students of different genders, races, and ages.

- Because time in section is precious, do not feel you have to work through the entire solution. If you know what caused the confusion, you can clarify that aspect of the problem and then allow students to complete their work independently.

- Remember: your goal is not simply to provide correct answers to the assigned problems but rather to foster your students' conceptual understanding.

Student Collaboration in Class

Students learn effectively from each other when working through problem sets. Different students understand different aspects and applications of concepts, and they can often explain them in ways their peers can understand. Do not hesitate to employ group learning during class.

Steps for Group Collaboration

1. Put students into groups of three or four students.
   See chapter 6, "Debate: Grouping Strategies," for more information on assigning students to groups.

2. Assign or hand out a set of problems and tell students how many problems they should try to do and how far along toward the answer they should try to get.

3. Walk around the room while students work and encourage them to work together, rather than sitting together and working alone. Feel free to sit down and participate in the solution of a problem, particularly if a group is struggling. Make yourself available to all groups to answer questions.

4. During the session, determine which groups have a solid understanding of which problems.

5. At the end of class, you can ask representatives from various groups to explain their solutions to the class. For example, one student can write out the problem on the board while another provides a "play-by-play" explanation.

Steps for Pair Collaboration

1. Put students into pairs.

2. Assign or hand out a set of problems and tell students how many problems they should try to do and how far along toward the answer they should try to get.

3. Have one student be the "talker" and the other be the "listener." The talker must explain to the listener (who can always ask questions) how they would work through a problem or set of problems.

4. Halfway through the session, you can have students switch roles.

5. Leave time at the end of class for a full-class review of at least a few problems. Choose one or more problems and ask the listeners to volunteer their partner if their partner provided a clear and detailed answer; if so, ask the talker to speak to the entire class (they have the advantage and confidence of having practiced the explanation once).

Guidelines for In-Class Collaboration

- Inevitably, some groups of students will contain classmates with similar levels of understanding, while other groups will have a wide range of abilities. It is important, therefore, that you keep reshuffling groups during the term so that students do not get trapped in particular roles within a group's dynamic (e.g., talker, listener).

- Find out your department's policy on encouraging and grading group work if the in-class work will be graded.

- Be very clear and explicit about what you expect and allow in terms of collaboration, both inside and outside of class. Students may come to your class with different expectations for how much collaboration is permissible on graded work.

- Be vigilant about keeping all group members engaged in the problem solving. Since they will be working individually on exams, they need to develop their own skills as well as their ability to work in groups.

- Some students work better alone and prefer to do their work that way. Different students benefit from different learning methods; you will be helpful to the greatest number of students if you vary your class plans from week to week.

Student Presentations

Student presentations reinforce the importance of risk taking and help create a learning community in which the process is valued as much as the product. Students can present completed problems to the class either on a spontaneous basis or with advance preparation.

Steps for Student Presentations

1. At the beginning of the term, establish a set number of points students will receive for a presentation (or credit that will go toward their participation grade). Tell students they always get full credit for a presentation as long as they have the material prepared; reinforce that they do not have to be correct but they do have to be prepared to talk through the solution. They must be able both to

re-create the solution on the board (or overhead projector) and to explain it as they go.

2. Tell students at the beginning of the term that they should be prepared to be corrected if necessary during their presentation in exchange for full presentation credit, given appropriate preparation. Again, you can remind students that they are working with difficult material and if they already had it perfectly mastered, they wouldn't be in the class. The key is the process and risk taking.

3. For a spontaneous student presentation ask the class if anyone is prepared to present a solution to a problem that another student has asked about. If so, turn over the front of the room to the student who feels prepared to present the solution. After you do this a few times, students will begin to prepare problems for presentation while they are doing their homework.

4. To organize students for prepared presentations of a problem set during the next session, ask which specific problems students do not understand or select a few problems you think will be particularly difficult for them. Then ask if there are any volunteers to present solutions for those problems in the next class. Make yourself available to those students for help before the next class so that they can feel confident making the presentation.

5. Once you turn over the front of the classroom to the student presenter, seat yourself near the front (perhaps off to one side) where you are available to help but not a dominant presence.

6. Be prepared to step in to correct mistakes if the presenter's classmates do not see the mistakes or are unwilling to correct them.

7. After a student presentation, thank the presenter for their work and, if applicable, point out strengths in their solution and presentation so that other students can identify key components of the process.

Guidelines for Student Presentations

- Alleviate as much anxiety as you can for student presenters by continually reinforcing that you see presentations as a useful way to assess student understanding.

- Stress that students always get full credit for the presentation as long as they have material prepared, even if the presentation is not perfect.

- Set yourself up as a support system for presentations, not a judge; students should know they can look to you for guidance if they are feeling lost or anxious during the presentation, particularly early in the term.

Eliciting Student Feedback

In-class questions obviously provide the most frequent and direct form of student feedback. You can also elicit feedback about how well students understand the material using one of the following "mini" lesson plans.

Sample Precinct

Choose a "sample precinct" (a row or a cluster of students). Admit that you are going to put them on the spot by asking them all a series of questions but make it clear that they are just the sample group. You are using these questions to assess overall class understanding, not to highlight their shortcomings and/or brilliance. Choose different precincts over the course of the term.

Initial Freewriting Activity

Ask students to take a few minutes at the beginning of class to write down what they recall from the last lecture or what they found confusing in the reading. Then ask for volunteers to share one of their responses; you can keep a list of the responses on the board. This activity can help provide continuity between lecture and section and help you focus your teaching on problem areas.

Final Freewriting Activity

Ask students to take a few minutes at the end of class to respond in writing to a question you ask. Depending on the question, you can make these responses anonymous or not.

Examples "Tell me what you now know about derivatives."

"Summarize for me what we talked about in class today."

"What concept is feeling the most confusing to you right now?"

"If we could review two things in class on Wednesday, what would they be?"

You can then use their answers to give students feedback about their progress or concerns as a class and to focus your teaching in the next class. Always read what they have written but do not feel compelled to respond individually (in writing or orally) to each student.

Grading Problem Sets

In math and in the sciences, exams are often graded on a curve, which can accurately and fairly reflect students' relative mastery of difficult material. With problem sets, you may want to dispense with a grading curve in order to encourage collaborative learning and create a more supportive learning community among the students. Find out your department's policy about encouraging and grading group work. Assuming group work is acceptable, encourage students to seek outside help (tutors, classmates, you); in the end, however, the work must be their own. Tell them you expect they will be able to explain the solution to *any* problem they answer. Remind them that they will be working individually on exams.

You may not have the power to determine how students are graded in section or to create extra graded assignments. If it is possible for you to develop a grading scheme, use quizzes (five- to ten-minute events) to encourage students to come to class prepared and to assess where students stand with respect to the material.

You can also consider developing a system that credits students for learning activities in which they demonstrate initiative, persistence, risk taking, and overall hard work. For example, you can create a system in which students receive credit for creating study sheets for exams (and turning them in), doing extra homework assignments or "stumper" problems, and giving class presentations. Enough credit at the end of the term can boost a borderline grade.

Running an Experimental Lab

Many courses in departments such as physics, biology, chemistry, or natural resources incorporate experimental labs into the teaching of the material. Teaching any particular lab requires a great deal of highly specific information and expertise in the relevant area. This section will address only general information applicable to experimental labs in most natural sciences.

Weekly Preparation

Many teaching assistants meet in weekly preparation sections with the course professor or laboratory instructor. In these sessions, the professor typically discusses the upcoming experiment, notes potential problems, and answers questions. The professor often addresses issues related to lab equipment, supplies, and safety. Use these sessions to familiarize yourself with the laboratory procedure and with the professor's expectations.

If it is possible, you should run each experiment yourself before your students come to the laboratory. This practice is time consuming, but it will save you a great deal of difficulty in the long run. Once you have worked through the experiment yourself, you will know

- exactly what equipment you will need for the day of the laboratory class;

- how much time students should allow for each part of the experiment;

- what material you can prepare as "backups" in case students fail to get the proper results in early stages of the experiment and their materials are unusable;

- which parts of the experiment are most likely to cause problems for students and how to fix them;

- what you should hope for in students' laboratory reports.

If it is impossible for you to run a laboratory experiment before the class meeting, carefully read the lab manual in advance and take note of the procedures or concepts that you cannot visualize without having run the experiment. Raise any questions you have during the preparatory session with the professor. Also, be sure to clarify these same points with your students; if it confused you, it will confuse them.

Laboratory Equipment

Prior to the first day of class, find time to go to the laboratory where you will be teaching. Make sure that you have the necessary access to the lab and to its materials. Check the equipment standard to the lab to see that it works. Even if the lab is in good working order, find out how to report equipment that needs to be repaired or replaced. For labs in which materials will be supplied on a weekly basis, find out who is responsible for maintaining and distributing the supplies and what teaching assistants are expected to do with regard to getting and returning supplies. Finally, locate the lab safety equipment (eye wash, fire extinguisher, etc.) and be sure that it is also in working order.

Laboratory Safety

Most laboratories involve a safety hazard of some kind. Be sure that you take time at the beginning of the semester to give your students clear instructions about the safety precautions of your laboratory. Once you have established the rules for safe laboratory procedures, enforce them vigilantly. If a student is being lax about safety (e.g., using a Bunsen burner for entertainment purposes) correct the student and alert them to the potential dangers of their behavior. If the student's dangerous behavior persists, you should—after appropriate warning—dismiss them from that particular lab and give them no credit for the lab or for the write-up.

Do not "bend" laboratory safety rules; if someone gets hurt under these circumstances, you will be held partly, if not fully, responsible. Be sure to lay out the laboratory safety rules and the consequences for breaking them in your syllabus. While it may feel like a hassle to send a student home when they show up wearing sandals or contact lenses to a chemistry laboratory that prohibits them, you are protecting the student and yourself by doing so.

Assigning Laboratory Groups

While some teaching assistants leave it to students to form their own groups, we recommend that you assign groups yourself according to the following guidelines.

- Separate friends; this often helps students stay focused on the task at hand, and it reduces opportunities for lab report plagiarism.

- To the degree that it is possible, evenly divide the men and women in your class among the laboratory groups. As science students are often predominantly male, you may find that your female students have trouble asserting themselves as equal partners in their groups. If this is the case, you may want to consider having some all-female groups.

- If you are aware that you have some students with more laboratory experience than others, you may want to pair them with less experienced students in order to ensure that most groups will finish the lab in a reasonable period of time. Make sure that the less experienced students are fully engaged and that the more experienced students are patient with them.

In extreme circumstances, students may need to switch lab groups. If such a situation arises, consult with the professor about how to approach the problem. You may be able to rearrange groups; you may have to move a student to another lab. Talk through with the professor how to present these changes to the students.

During the Laboratory

It is often effective to write an outline of the experiment steps on the board before class begins. When students arrive, talk them through the steps of the experiment and ask what questions they have about the procedure. Also, remind students of the aim of the lab and how it is relevant to lecture material. Once the experiment is under way, walk around the lab continuously and check in with each group. Students are far more likely to ask you important questions if you come to them than if you are sitting at a desk, away from the main activity of the lab. This also increases the energy level of the class and makes the whole thing more fun for everyone.

Answering Questions and Correcting Mistakes

When students have questions about the lab experiment, or when they are struggling with an experimental procedure, do not come to the rescue right away. Keep in mind that lab experiments are a vehicle through which students are taught about scientific methods and principles; it is far more important that your students understand the "big picture" behind a given experiment than that they achieve perfect experimental results. Student experiments have already been simplified and distilled to the level where they are manageable in a few hours. It can be important for students to see that experiments derail, that the next step is not always clear, and that decisions about how to proceed depend on the goal of the experiment.

Relate specific questions from your students to their broader understanding of the goals of the lab and ask them to make specific experimental decisions with this "bigger picture" in mind. Encourage students to work together to figure out an answer or how to get back on track with the experiment. Ask your students questions that will guide their thinking toward the information they need. Offer answers only when absolutely necessary.

EXAMPLE   "So, your bacteria didn't grow. Think of all the reasons why bacteria might not grow. Which ones might apply here?"

Keeping Students on Track and Involved

Experimental labs often involve periods of waiting between different phases of an experiment. You can use this time to engage students in question and answer periods designed to develop their understanding of the larger lesson behind any particular experiment. Ask your students questions that test their understanding of how the different parts of the lab experiment are related to the overall goals of the lab. You can also ask them questions about the lecture or present them with data or other information with which they have to generate a hypothesis. The point is to keep them immersed in the process of mastering the scientific method.

You are also likely to come across students who are happy to let their lab partners work on the experiment while they work on the crossword puzzle. This can be especially tricky when there really are more lab group members than tasks for particular parts of an experiment. Make a point of asking a crossword puzzler questions about the lab: what their partners are working on, the importance of this step in the experiment, and so on. Show students that you expect them to be fully involved in the lab and to understand what is happening, even if they have no specific task at that moment.

Wrapping up the Lab

Because different lab groups will complete the experiment at different times, it is often impossible to give a final summary statement about the point of the lab. Instead, try to meet with each group of students as they are finishing to see how their experiment went and to answer questions they may have about how to summarize their findings in their lab reports. If necessary, you might want to institute a "formal" procedure in which groups are required to check in with you before leaving. This is also a good time to make sure that each lab group is cleaning up their equipment and returning their work space to its original condition.

Common Problems in Labs

It is unlikely that you will get through a single semester of teaching in a laboratory without facing at least one of the problems listed here.

Failed Experiments

For one reason or another, you will have a lab group whose experiment fails to achieve any semblance of the desired results. When this happens, remind your students that they can still do well on their lab reports. Instruct them to explain carefully why their experiment failed to achieve the expected results, to be frank about the shortcomings in their methods, and to take their experimental difficulties into account when interpreting any results they did achieve. Be sure to use failed experiments as a learning opportunity: ask students to generate hypotheses for their odd results and then describe how they would test these hypotheses to see what really went wrong. In this way a "failed" lab becomes another way to learn about the scientific method.

Students Who Miss Lab

Establish your policy on missed labs at the beginning of the semester and write it on the syllabus. Because it is nearly impossible to "make up" a missed lab, you need to be clear with your students about how you plan to handle such absences.

Inattentive Students

While very inattentive students only hurt themselves in most classrooms, they can be a serious detriment to a laboratory group. While you can expect an inattentive student's classmates to exert some pressure on the student to do their share, you should not place the burden of motivating an unmotivated student entirely upon the other students in their group. You should address this kind of situation as early in the semester as possible.

Watch for students who are often (or always) reading the newspaper or chatting while the rest of their lab group is hard at work. During class, encourage the inattentive student to become involved in the work of the group.

EXAMPLE　　"Maria, the rest of your group looks busy; find out from them what you should be doing."

You need to catch this kind of behavior as early as you can. Once a group of students identifies a member as "dead weight" they will often respond by isolating that student and figuring out how to work efficiently without them. At that point, it is more difficult for the student to be reintegrated into the group. If this behavior persists, schedule a meeting with the student outside of class to remind them of how their performance in the lab will affect their grade.

Lab Reports

Once the lab is over, your students face the challenge of summarizing and explaining their results in a lab report. While students will learn to write better lab reports from trial and error, you can speed the learning process by offering some important information at the beginning of the term.

Explain the Purpose of Lab Reports

Students will often assume that you want them to mold their lab results—and their lab report—to what they think *should* have happened during the lab. Explain to students that experiments are as much about process as results. Tell students that it is possible to receive an A on a lab report summarizing a "failed" experiment and that students can also receive an F for a report on an experiment that went very well.

What matters in the lab report is that students demonstrate their understanding of what was *supposed* to have happened in the lab, *why* it was supposed to have happened, and *how* their own results were achieved (even if their results are wrong!). Again, stress to your students that labs are designed to familiarize them with the scientific methods and principles of their field; the lab reports should be used to demonstrate their understanding of both.

Clarify Your Expectations

Tell your students in detail what format you prefer for lab reports: the necessary sections to include; how formal the writing should be; if reports may be handwritten; how many decimal places should be allowed for numerical results; if they may write their entire reports on graph paper; approximately how long a report should be; and so on. Describe explicitly what goes in each section; it is a somewhat artificial way of organizing things, so students need a lot of guidance. Lab reports present a significant challenge to many students; take out as much of the "guesswork" about what you expect as you possibly can.

Also, be very clear with students (preferably on your course syllabus) about the penalties for late lab reports.

See chapter 2, "Syllabus: Setting the Agenda," for more information on establishing policies for the class.

Teach from Old Lab Reports

At the beginning of the term, make copies of old lab reports that students can use as models for their own reports (make sure they describe experiments your students will not be doing!). Review these reports with students and highlight the strengths and weaknesses of each report. Again, help your students to see the "big picture" behind lab experimentation and to appreciate how they can use their lab reports to communicate their understanding of how their results are related to the goals of the lab. Talk with students about *why* lab reports are set up according to a particular format—why all the included information is important for them as scientists.

Group Lab Reports

There are benefits and drawbacks to asking students to write group lab reports.

Pros   Students learn more about working in groups.

It involves less grading for you.

Students can pool their knowledge.

Cons   It may be difficult to ascertain the understanding of individual group members.

It may discourage active lab participation by all members of the group.

Some students may do almost no work, while others will do the lion's share.

See chapter 8, "Grading Group Work," for more information on how to grade group assignments.

You may want to alternate assignments, asking students to write some lab reports individually and some in groups.

Teach from New Lab Reports

Each week, you can ask one group to prepare a presentation for the next lab in which they give an oral lab report (with a much reduced Methods section). This allows the class as a whole to sum up the previous lab and discuss problems or theoretical issues. It also keeps students from forgetting (quite so immediately!) what they did last week.

Further Reading

Clarke, J., and A. Biddle, eds. 1993. *Teaching Critical Thinking: Reports from across the Curriculum.* Englewood Cliffs, NJ: Prentice Hall.

Davidson, N., ed. 1990. *Cooperative Learning in Mathematics: A Handbook for Teachers.* Menlo Park, CA: Addison-Wesley.

McKeachie, W. J., and M. Svinicki. 2006. *McKeachie's Teaching Tips: Strategies, Research, and Theory for College and University Teachers.* 12th ed. Boston: Houghton Mifflin.

Seymour, E. 1997. *Talking about Leaving: Why Undergraduates Leave the Sciences.* Boulder, CO: Westview Press.

Tobias, S. 1992. *Revitalizing Undergraduate Science: Why Some Things Work and Most Things Don't.* Tucson, AZ: Research Corp.

Chapter 6
Trusty Class Plans

Some course material and class goals lend themselves to more highly structured class plans—more structured than the typical full-class discussion. This chapter provides nine tried-and-true plans, which cover a range of different goals and activities.

Information Exchange

For information exchange students read an assigned segment of course material at home and then present a summary of the readings in class to their classmates.

When to Use It

Information exchanges work very well when you are trying to cover a lot of information quickly and you think that students may not be doing all the reading (or at least not doing all of it very carefully). You are, in a sense, organizing a class study session, and it is often better to have the students learn the information this way than (1) have you lecture to them about it or (2) not learn it at all.

Students can teach each other, and they often learn a lot from it. You are not shirking your duties if students run the class according to a structure you have planned; you already have done plenty of work to create that situation. Smaller informational exchanges can be organized and completed in one class period, but it is usually more effective to have students prepare ahead of time so that they are ready to teach their classmates when they walk into class.

Advance Preparation for the Teaching Assistant

If students are supposed to read, for example, four articles that week, divide the class (or a subsection of the class) into four groups the week before (see "Debate" in this chapter for grouping strategies). Assign each group an article and tell them that the next week they will have a certain amount of time (say, fifteen minutes) to help their classmates get the most out of that article. (Remind them that they must read all the articles; they will get more out of the next class if they do.) It often works well to require each group to have a handout for their classmates: it can summarize relevant information, provide questions for other students to answer, list important terms, and so forth. Tell them that if they get it to you the day before, you will copy it and have it ready for class.

Advance Preparation for Students

When you do this activity for the first time, prepare students for their fifteen minutes of teaching. Remind them that talking *at* their peers is not interesting and it will be much livelier if they can get the other students involved. Go so far as to suggest activities, such as pair work you have done as a class before, freewriting, or creating lists. Encourage them to make handouts that you will copy before class. Make yourself available to meet with the groups during office hours to go over their teaching plans. It also helps to remind students that they will be graded on the quality of their presentations.

Steps for an Information Exchange

1. Tell groups in what order they will present. You can organize this thematically or draw numbers out of a hat.

2. Have the presenting group move to the front of the room where they command attention. It never hurts to have students move around, and it makes them seem more like the leaders of the class.

3. Keep very close track of time so that you can get to all the presentations. You may want to make a warning "five minutes left" sign to flash at the presenters.

Wrapping Up

At the end of class, you need to synthesize all this information into a more coherent whole. Take a few minutes and talk to students about how their presentations fit together in a larger scheme and what the most important points are. This is a very appropriate time to lecture; they have not heard your voice for the entire class, and even with good presentations, the students need to understand how the pieces fit together. And be sure to compliment them specifically on a job well done. Even when there are shortcomings in the presentations, you need to point out where students have succeeded. Students need to hear a balance of constructive criticism and encouragement from you.

Debate

When to Use It

Debates encourage students to challenge each other's and their own thinking about controversial issues. While debating may seem like a gimmick, the ability to take information and construct a coherent, compelling argument is at the heart of a liberal arts education. Debates may be especially useful in cases in which you think that your students already have firm positions on an issue or when you want to encourage them to make a thoughtful argument for their position. Debates are also a good way for students to hear both sides of an argument where a full discussion might be stifled by students' efforts to be politically correct. Debates are an excellent option when you want to spend less time preparing for class (e.g., during your own academic crunch periods).

Advance Preparation for the Teaching Assistant

To have a debate, you will need to divide students into two groups, each of which will argue for a particular position on the topic you choose. Before the debate, you will need to decide the topic and how you will divide your students into groups.

EXAMPLES   Should marijuana be legalized?

Should animals be used for testing possible human immunizations?

Should U.S. citizens not born in the United States be allowed to run for president?

Advance Preparation for Students

You may want to remind your students to bring informational materials to class or to examine specific readings before class on the day you are planning to hold a debate. But, because debating can seem like a corny exercise, you may want to wait until the day you are planning to hold a debate to tell students about this class plan. The longer they know about it, the longer they have to decide that they may not feel like participating.

Grouping Strategies

Here are several different strategies for dividing students into groups.

- Divide students into groups by having them number off. This can have the advantage of separating friends who usually sit next to each other in class into different groups. Separating friends is a good idea if you suspect that they will not stay on task or challenge each other's ideas if assigned to the same group.

- Decide before class which students you would like in each group. This method gives you an opportunity to create groups of students who you think will work well together and to put at least one good talker in each group.

- Ask students to divide themselves into two groups. This method may take more time than you want to spend, as students can be slow to take initiative on this type of task.

- Divide the classroom down the middle. This method is efficient, but it gives you less control over who ends up in each group. The advantage of "natural grouping" is that in these groups, students are already comfortable talking among themselves.

Steps for Debates

1. Start by telling the class that you will begin today's discussion with a debate.

2. Divide the students into two groups. Once they are in groups, ask each group to pick a "secretary" to record the group's ideas. Assign each group a position with regard to the debate topic.

3. Give them ten minutes to work together to come up with all of the arguments that they can on behalf of their position. Remind the secretary to take notes.

4. Give the groups a two minute warning so they know when they need to start wrapping up.

5. Pick one of the groups to start the debate and instruct the group that will be going first that it is to make the first point by stating and explaining one of its arguments for or against the issue at hand. For example, the first group might say, "Marijuana should be legalized because it can be used to treat some medical disorders," and then briefly explain this position. Groups should select one or two speakers for each point.

6. Instruct the second group that they are to confer with each other and respond to the first group's point. Once the second group responds, give the first group the opportunity to comment on the response.

7. Once the first point has been exhausted, ask the second group to offer a new point.

Throughout this process, it is your job to keep the debate running smoothly. Be sure the groups take turns in making and rebutting points and that no one group or student dominates the debate. You should decide when a point has been exhausted and when to raise a new one.

You also may encourage the students to take turns speaking for their group. For example, the members of each group may take turns stating each point or rebuttal. Be sure to give the groups time to confer with each other before they make or rebut a point if they need the time to consolidate their argument.

Once the debate is under way, you may go one of two ways with it. You do not need to decide in advance; see how the debate is progressing.

Option One

8. Continue the process of point making, responding, and rebutting for five to ten minutes. Allow this to go on long enough for each group to become involved in arguing carefully for its position but stop the debate *before* a majority of the important points have been raised.

9. Stop the debate, instruct the groups to reconvene, and ask each group to prepare to argue the opposite position of the one they just argued.

10. Give the groups five minutes to work out the opposing position and then start the debate in the same manner as before.

11. Allow the debate to continue as long as the groups are making thoughtful points but leave at least ten minutes at the end of class to wrap up.

By forcing the students to take the position opposite of the one they just debated, you expand their thinking and almost certainly force them to challenge some of the ideas they held before class. The downside of this format is that it can cut into a smoothly flowing debate.

Option Two

8. Allow the debate to continue until the groups make most of the significant points related to the issue at hand.

9. Stop the debate before your students seem bored with it or the debate activity begins to drag.

When students do not have to change their position on the issue, they may be able to think through one position thoroughly. In addition, by not stopping the debate midway, you allow it to follow a more natural course. The downside of this format is that your students may leave the classroom without challenging their own thinking about the issue.

Your decision to follow option one or option two may rest on the students' familiarity with the material. Decide if the goal of the class is to generate as many ideas on the topic as possible or to generate a coherent, point-by-point argument on the topic.

Wrapping Up

After you stop the debate, have your students move back into their regular classroom positions. To help them reflect on the results of the debate, you have a few different options.

- Ask your students if they were surprised by any of the arguments or if they have changed their own views on the topic.

- Have your students go through the various points and group the arguments under appropriate headings. As you do this, explain to students how they can apply a similar process when constructing the argument for a paper.

- Have your students pick out fallacious or circular arguments. Find out why they think people would make those weak arguments.

- Focus on the politically incorrect arguments. Who makes these arguments? Are they completely wrong, or do they have elements of truth?

- Find the arguments that oppose each other. Talk about the importance of addressing opposing arguments when making a point.

- Find arguments without any clear opposition and discuss how you would argue against them.

- Acknowledge that these are complex issues that can have reasoned and thoughtful opposing arguments.

Pros and Cons

When to Use It

This is a particularly good exercise to use when you want to bring out a variety of opinions about a controversial topic but you do not have enough time or energy to stage a debate. Pros and Cons can be used to jump-start what you hope will be a more free-flowing discussion. Like debating, Pros and Cons allows students to voice a variety of opinions (even those that are not politically correct) without worrying about being held personally accountable for their views.

Advance Preparation for the Teaching Assistant

Before doing Pros and Cons in your classroom, you need to think of a controversial issue and write down in your class plan arguments on both sides of the issue. As with debates, pros and cons can help students see the many complex sides of an issue on which they may already have taken a firm position, thus helping them construct a more thoughtful, persuasive argument.

Advance Preparation for Students

The amount of preparation your students will need depends on the topic you have in mind. If you are covering a topic about which students will benefit from having factual information available to them (e.g., "Should Puerto Rico be made a U.S. State?"), you should encourage your students to review certain materials before they come to class. If you are covering a topic with which students are already familiar, you won't need to give them advance warning.

Steps for Pros and Cons

1. Divide the board in half, and write PRO on one side and CON on the other.

2. Tell your students the controversial issue that you have in mind and ask them to come up with all of the arguments that someone might make for or against the issue. You can ask them to do this in pairs first and then share with the full class, or you can work with the full class.

3. Be sure that you ask students to give you all of the available arguments, as opposed to asking them their opinions on the topic. This way, students will be liberated to say things that they might otherwise worry will be held against them personally.

4. Write the arguments on the board as they are given to you by the students. Keep your own list in front of you so that you can add important points that the students leave out. You may have to make the first politically incorrect comment in order to get that side of the issue "on the board." If you find your class tiptoeing around politically charged issues, be the first to say, for example, "Well, some people feel that Puerto Rico should not be made a state because most of its citizens are minorities."

5. Continue until you feel both sides of the issue have been exhausted.

Wrapping Up

Once you have extensive lists for both sides of the issue, point out to your students that this is the process through which meaningful arguments (e.g., papers) are composed. They can use a similar process to generate ideas, choose a position, and organize an argument while considering plausible counterarguments. See "Wrapping Up" under "Debate" in this chapter for a list of suggested closing activities. The advantage with this class plan is that you have all the ideas on the board so that you can physically connect or group them with your chalk or pen.

Consolidating Lists

When to Use It

When you have a question with discrete, "listable" answers, this class plan can be an effective way to generate discussion. It works particularly well with a topic that seems at first glance too abstract to define but that can, in fact, be characterized (e.g., good writing). This exercise also helps students sift through and prioritize ideas and arguments. It is inherently artificial to ask students to come up with a certain number of answers; it is perfectly appropriate for you to recognize that fact when you introduce the activity, but it is not a reason to dismiss the exercise.

Examples   List ten characteristics of good writing.

List five possible arguments against the English Language Amendment.

List six potential flaws in a sociological study like the one in the article.

Advance Preparation for the Teaching Assistant

All you need to do ahead of time is think of the question, decide how many points to put on the list, and decide how many times you want to consolidate lists. You should also make your own list in your class plan so that you can be sure that students cover all of the points you think are important.

Steps for Consolidating Lists

1. Ask each student to get out a piece of paper and explain the list you would like them to create.

2. Give them five to ten minutes to complete their lists.

3. When all of the students have lists, put them in pairs and tell them to consolidate their two lists into one with the original number of items. They must, therefore, decide which items can be combined and which items are more important than others.

4. Optional: next, put the pairs into groups of four and ask them to consolidate the two lists into one. At this point, they will begin to identify common threads. You also can ask them to rank these elements in order of importance.

Wrapping Up

The easiest way to bring this exercise back to a full-class discussion is to create a class list on the board. With you as the transcriber, ask each group to provide one or two items for the master list. Once you reach the designated number, ask for additional items; as a class, determine whether they should displace or be combined with an item already on the board. When the list is finished, you can talk to the class about how this exercise proves how much shared knowledge we do or do not possess about what is important or characteristic of this given issue.

You also can use any of the suggested activities in "Wrapping Up" under "Debate" in this chapter.

Video Presentation

Before you plan the viewing of a video into your syllabus, check with the media center at your institution to learn the policy for showing films in the classroom for educational purposes.

When to Use It

Showing a video or a movie can bring a perspective into your classroom that is not available in other ways. Your goal can be purely informational (a documentary about South African politics), to provide a needed example (a feature film with an excellent example of psychopathology), or to introduce a novel viewpoint (labor relations from the perspective of the union workers' families).

Advance Preparation for the Teaching Assistant

Watch the movie or program at least once before showing it to the class. Be sure it will fit into the time allotted. If not, determine what parts you can skip. Decide which points or themes you think the students should focus on as they watch. Prepare questions for your students that fit the goal you had in mind when you chose the video material; you can either put these questions on a handout that you distribute at the beginning of class or keep them for a full-class discussion after the video.

Reserve the necessary equipment: TV, VCR, and so forth. Get to class early that day to make sure everything is there and working.

Advance Preparation for Students

Unfortunately, some students think of a day with video material as a nonrequired class. Tell your students that you will be showing a video at least a week before you plan to do so and explain why it is important for them to see it (this way, they will not see the projector and turn tail). Your job is to show and enforce for students how these programs or films are educational, because students' immediate reaction will be to leave or, if they stay, to sit back, relax, turn off their brains, and enjoy the show. In the week before, you should mention some incentive for watching the video carefully (an assignment, the final exam, etc.).

Steps for a Video Presentation

1. You will want to introduce the video material either in the previous class or just prior to showing the movie or both. Remember, it is your responsibility to frame this as an educational experience. Tell them about the director, the making of the production, its relevance to the course, and so on.

2. If possible, help students to watch and talk about the video critically. Ask students to take notes during the movie or write down their reflections afterward in response to questions from your handout. You also can ask students to write responses to the movie for homework (either general responses or responses to a specific question that you pose).

Wrapping Up

A postvideo discussion can cover questions from the handout or questions that you prepared in advance. This is also a good time to talk about how useful students found the video, if they felt that it challenged or expanded their thinking, and how you envisioned the video enhancing other course material.

Guest Speaker

When to Use Them

Guest speakers are especially helpful when you are dealing with a topic that would be enhanced by the perspective of someone who has very specific experience in the area. Depending on your field, a guest speaker might be a fellow graduate student who does research in the area of interest, the director of the local recycling plant, a dissident from a country discussed in your course, or an ex-convict. Be creative when thinking about the kind of speakers who could enhance the teaching in your course!

Advance Preparation for the Teaching Assistant

You will want to invite only guest speakers who will be able to speak thoughtfully and effectively in front of your students. Although you may know a fascinating person who is also an accomplished environmentalist, you will not want to invite them to speak to your class on natural resources if they are painfully shy in front of groups. Often, you will be able to find guest speakers who are accustomed to speaking to large groups, but if you have any concerns about the person you would like to invite, do not hesitate to ask them how they feel about speaking in front of thirty students for an hour.

Once you have selected a guest speaker, talk with them about what kind of presentation will work for your class. Be sure to cover these points:

- how long the guest speaker will speak (e.g., the entire class period, only fifteen minutes);
- how their talk fits in with the structure of the course;
- whether they should be prepared to answer questions from your students;
- what your students already know about the topic;
- particular interests your students have expressed.

Advance Preparation for Students

Let your students know in advance when you will have a guest speaker. If you plan to have the speaker take questions from students, have your students write questions as a homework assignment before the speaker arrives. This forces the students to prepare for the presentation, allows you to ensure that there are questions, and can help your speaker to prepare their presentation. Also, remind your students that the speaker is a guest of the class, so, *of course,* they will arrive at class on time and give the speaker their full attention for the duration of the period.

Steps for a Class with a Guest Speaker

1. Begin class by dealing with minor class business (if necessary) and then introduce the speaker. Tell students the format for the presentation (e.g., whether there will be time left at the end of class for questions).

2. Turn the class over to the guest speaker. Your advance preparation with the guest speaker should make for a thoughtful, appropriate, and interesting presentation. If it turns out that your guest speaker is pitching their talk too high, too low, or in the wrong place altogether, you must wait patiently until a natural break occurs in the presentation for an opportunity to help the speaker focus on the useful subjects for your class.

3. If questions from the class or a whole-class discussion are included as part of the presentation, it is your job to call on students or to moderate the discussion unless the speaker indicates otherwise. It is always a good idea to have a few questions of your own prepared in case the discussion needs a jump start.

4. It is your job to end class on time. When the end of class arrives, thank your speaker for coming and tell your students to hold any unanswered questions; you can find time in the following week to discuss them as a class.

Wrapping Up

It is always a good idea to send your guest speaker a note thanking them for their contributions to your class. If time and logistics allow, bring a card with you to the following class and have your students sign the thank-you note before you send it.

In the first class meeting after you have had a guest speaker, ask your students what they thought about the presentation, what they found useful, surprising, or unsettling. While you may want to put a time limit on this discussion so that you can get on to the rest of your class plan, it is important to get feedback from your students about the speaker before you think about whether to invite the same speaker back next semester.

Exam Preparation

When to Use It

If you plan to devote all or most of a class to preparing your students for an exam, do so in the last class meeting before an exam is administered. Although it would be wonderful to help students prepare for an exam two weeks in advance, it is not practical. It is a rare college student who begins to study for an exam more than a few days before they have to take it.

Some teaching assistants feel that they are pandering to grade-grubbing students when they devote class time to exam preparation, but taking time for this kind of review is exactly the purpose of giving exams in the first place. Exams provide an excellent opportunity to encourage students to consolidate and synthesize what they have learned in your course by capitalizing on their motivation to do well on the exam. In addition, exam taking is an academic skill like any other. When you teach students exam preparation skills, you help them recognize and remember what is important in your course.

Advance Preparation for the Teaching Assistant

You will need to go over all the material that will be covered on the exam to make sure that it all makes sense to you. If you choose option one from the following group of options, make copies of an old exam to hand out to your students in the class meeting before the exam preparation session. If you choose option two, leave time to create a handout of student questions.

Advance Preparation for Students

How you ask students to prepare for the exam preparation session will dictate how you run the session itself. Choose one or two options that will work best for the material you will review.

Option One

If you have copies of old exams that are similar to the one you will administer, ask your students to work through the old exams before the exam preparation session and take note of areas where they have difficulty. If you are uncomfortable giving out an old exam, check to see if students have access to one anyway. Many fraternities, sororities, and other student groups save old exams. In this case, not distributing an old exam may only penalize students with poor access.

Option Two

Before the exam preparation session, ask students to go through the material the exam will cover and write three questions they would ask if they were writing the exam. They must get these questions to you (in your box or by e-mail) two days before the preparation session.

Option Three

Before the exam preparation session, have your students go through the material and come up with specific questions about areas that they do not understand. Tell your students that you will be happy to clarify any topic for them but that you will not answer questions like "What parts of the text do you think we should study?"

With any of these three options, you can spend part of the class period talking with students about test-taking strategies. For example, you can talk over with students how to write a successful in-class essay (e.g., foregrounding your main point), what counts as "explaining the significance" of a passage in an identification section, and so on. Many of them will probably be willing to share their successful (or dramatically unsuccessful!) strategies both for studying and for taking similar exams.

Steps for Exam Preparation

The steps that you use for your exam preparation session will depend on the options you chose from those listed previously.

Option One

1. Give your students the correct answers to the sample exam on a handout. Or have pairs of students compare their answers to look for discrepancies.

2. Have your students ask specific questions about areas where they struggled on the sample exam.

3. Encourage students to help each other toward the correct answers and clarify any controversies about the material. If no one in the class seems to know a given answer, give the answer to the class. Even if similar material will be covered on the upcoming exam, what counts is that the students learn and remember it!

4. Work through as many questions as you can in the time available.

Option Two

1. Have a handout prepared with as many of the students' questions as you feel are appropriate (you may need to consolidate some questions or add a few of your own).

2. Put students in groups of three or four to work through the questions together. Be available to answer groups' questions as they go.

3. Bring the discussion back to the full class to go over questions that caused trouble.

4. Finally, ask students to volunteer additional questions that did not come up and go over them as a class.

Option Three

1. Begin class by reminding your students that you will limit the preparation session to answering specific questions; your students should not expect you to summarize the exam material for them.

2. Field questions from your students one at a time. Solicit input from the class on each question but answer questions where no one has the correct answer or if too much time will be spent on getting the correct answer.

3. Continue to take questions on the exam material for as long as the class period allows, or until they run out of specific questions.

Wrapping Up

Regardless of the option you choose, you will want to keep track of the topics that are addressed in the exam preparation session and note any areas of the material that will be on the exam that were not adequately addressed in the preparation session. Remind students about these important topics and encourage them to study those areas also.

Grammar and Usage Review

When to Use It

In a course in which you are reading student writing, you may find yourself becoming frustrated by recurring usage problems. This activity is a quick and easy way to review and correct common usage mistakes.

When you do this exercise, you can remind students that part of "good grammar" is mastering a set of written conventions. The written language differs from the spoken, and your students may not always be able to find a logic to a particular written convention; but in many contexts, they will be judged by their control of these grammatical usage rules. Setting up written grammar in this way can make this exercise seem more like a challenging game than a test of the students' intellect or fluency.

Advance Preparation for the Teaching Assistant

Select eight to ten sentences from your students' writing that exemplify the problems you want to tackle. You may need to alter students' sentences slightly or make up a couple of examples. Using actual student writing makes the exercise seem less abstract, and students usually find the usage issues in their own writing to be more amusing than embarrassing (and the sentences are anonymous unless a student opts to claim ownership during class).

Keep the sentences fairly short so that the students do not become distracted from the targeted usage questions. Choose your sentences thematically: do not try to cover ten different usage problems; select two or three problems instead (e.g., comma splices, lack of parallelism, dangling modifiers) and use the sentences to cover different variations of these problems.

Type these sentences onto a handout (without the student authors' names). Make sure to leave space between the sentences so that students can add their corrections.

> ## Sentence Revision (a.k.a. Usage Questions)
>
> *Revise the following sentences so that they are clear and no longer contain usage problems. (Some of these sentences should look familiar!)*
>
> 1. The comparison of two simultaneous trials should identify any idiosyncratic problems with the sample collection, this methodology helps to ensure more accurate results.
> 2. The artist captures the serenity of the scene in the diffusion of soft colors; although the overlaid short brush strokes imbue the painting with living vitality.
> 3. The governor has tried to defend his actions, however, his press secretary has tried to pretend the incident never occurred.

Steps for Grammar and Usage Review

1. Explain to the students why you have decided they will benefit from a review of usage questions and explicitly give them a time limit for the exercise if you are planning to cover other material that day.

2. Give each student a copy of the handout and have them revise the sentences in pairs. This strategy allows students to compare grammatical knowledge and answer some of their own questions.

3. While students are working, put numbers on the board for the number of sentences on the handout, leaving space for students to write the corrected sentences.

4. After five minutes, walk around the room and ask various pairs to have one partner put a revised version of the sentence on the board when they are ready.

5. As a class, go over the revised versions of the sentences. Ask students for other possible revisions or for other questions that come to mind.

6. If time allows, ask students what other grammatical issues have been giving them trouble.

Wrapping Up

Tell students that you expect never to see any of these problems again in their writing. They laugh, you laugh, and you hope that at least they understand a little more about usage conventions than they did before they walked into the classroom. Then move on to the next class activity.

Paper Workshop

When to Use It

If students are writing a paper for your class and you want to emphasize the process of writing (drafts and revision), workshops are an effective way to make students put more time into their writing. Students work in small groups (three or four students) to help each other improve their drafts. They will have read the papers beforehand and made written comments, so the workshop involves talking about the drafts rather than reading them.

Advance Preparation for the Teaching Assistant

You must create workshop groups; you can announce these when you give the paper assignment. Groups of three work best, but groups of four are possible. The directions that follow assume your students will be working in groups of three. If you know the students' writing, try to put at least one strong writer in each group to act both as a model for the other students and as a trusty peer responder.

Before the first workshop, you should provide guidelines about how students should compose their written responses to drafts of other students' essays and about how the workshop is supposed to run.

Create a schedule of due dates: draft due date (when students will give their drafts to the other members of their group); workshop date (a few days after the draft due date, when students will come prepared with their written responses to the two other papers in their group); final paper due date.

Emphasize to students their responsibility for the success of this activity. They must have their drafts ready, and they must be present in class for the workshop. You may want to stress repercussions for missing the workshop, as this will inevitably doom the group's effectiveness and is not fair to the student's peers.

If the draft due date is a class day, have students exchange papers at the beginning or end of class. If the draft due date has to be a nonclass day, make sure that students have each other's e-mail addresses and phone numbers so that they can contact each other and make the exchange.

Before the first workshop, go over with students how the workshop should unfold. You may want to hold a practice full-class workshop with an essay from another class you have taught or from another teaching assistant so that students can see how a workshop should progress; you can ask one student to pretend to be the author (or volunteer yourself) so that the other students direct their (sensitive and constructive) comments to an "author figure." Encourage them to provide positive comments along with constructive suggestions. You can also provide written workshop guidelines for students.

See appendix E for a sample set of written guidelines and further information about how to run a paper workshop.

Advance Preparation for Students

Students must have the drafts of their papers prepared by the draft due date and should bring three copies of their draft to class that day: one for themselves and one for each of the other people in their workshop group. You may opt to have them make a copy for you also but be very clear about whether you are planning to read it or whether you are simply checking to make sure they have written it.

Students will take the other two students' papers home and write a peer response to each, commenting on the argument, tone, organization, and so forth. When students come to class on the day of the workshop, they will bring two copies of each response: one for the student writer and one for you (you probably will want to grade these responses so that students put time and effort into them).

Provide students with a set of guidelines about how to write these responses to other students' essays. Emphasize that they should focus first on the big issues (the argument, organization) and only later on punctuation and grammar (if it even becomes relevant). Explain how long the response should be (one to two pages works well) and how you will grade it.

See appendix F for a sample set of guidelines for writing a peer response.

Steps for Paper Workshops

1. On the day of the workshop, have all students pull out their copy of their own papers. Ask them to take a few minutes and write on

the top of their papers three questions they would like to ask their peer responders (e.g., "How can I fix the conclusion?").

2. Put the students into their groups, remind them of their task, and let them go at it. Tell them about how long they should spend on each paper. Encourage them to look at their drafts of and responses to the one student's paper but not to read their written responses verbatim to the student; the student can read the responses at home later—the workshop is a time for two-way dialogue.

3. Walk around the room and keep an eye on the progress of all the groups. Feel free to join in a group for a few minutes if they seem to be struggling or having a disagreement.

Wrapping Up

When all the groups have finished discussing the papers, remind students of the due date for the final draft. If you are willing to meet with students about their papers before then, you may want to stipulate that they must revise the draft after the workshop before they talk to you about it.

Grading

You will want to grade the written responses to ensure that students put some time and care into them—you may want to use grades or a simple number system (e.g., 1–5). If you choose to collect the first drafts, you will have to decide whether you want to grade these for effort or simply to refer to them when grading the final versions. Obviously, students benefit from getting your written feedback on paper drafts, but there are serious downsides to doing so.

- Reading and commenting on two drafts of a paper takes an inordinate amount of your time.

- Students may dismiss their peers' comments on the draft, waiting only for your comments.

- Students often believe that if they respond to all of your written comments on the draft (and no more), they will get an A. As this is often not the case, they may feel misled.

An effective alternative for helping students with paper drafts is arranging individual meetings with students during your office hours to discuss their papers. You can offer to skim through drafts and provide general feedback that will help students rewrite their work.

An Optional Final Class Exercise for a Paper Workshop

Most students make no distinction between revising and editing. The workshop will help them to see that revision can involve a structural overhaul, the addition or subtraction of ideas, the reworking of the introduction, and so forth. If you want to teach them a lesson about editing—about the importance of proofreading for good presentation— try this exercise.

Steps for this Final Exercise

1. On the day the paper is due, pair up students and have them exchange papers. (They will groan, but you can explain that if any- one has a perfect paper at the end of the class, you will be happy to take it. If not, they have a chance to fix it.)

2. Ask them to proofread each other's papers for grammar and punc- tuation. Ask every student to give their partner permission to write on their paper. Encourage them to go slowly, to read aloud if they want to.

3. Provide them with a proofreading guide sheet of common problems if you have one prepared.

4. Make yourself available for any and all usage questions that may arise.

5. Determine whether anyone has an unmarked paper. If so, collect it. If not, tell the students that they have until the next day to fix the problems and get the paper into your mailbox.

This exercise works wonderfully the first time because students are not expecting it and they come to class with final drafts. Once the ele- ment of surprise is gone, however, they tend to use this editing session as a second revision session, and they do not come prepared with final drafts.

Proofreading Guide Sheet

Here is a list of some common problems to watch for when you *edit* your draft, *after* you have *revised* it:

1. This/That   When these words stand alone at the beginning of a sentence, their reference is often unclear; putting a noun after "this" or "that" (e.g., "this fact" or "this situation") will help make the reference clear.

2. Verb tense   Pay attention to verb tense. Do not change tense randomly.

3. Comma splices   Commas cannot connect two independent clauses alone (semicolons can).

4. You   If you use "you" in the paper, make sure that you have a reason for directly addressing the audience at that particular point in the paper.

(And so on)

Further Reading

Cannon, R., and D. Newble. 2000. *A Handbook for Teachers in Universities and Colleges: A Guide to Improving Teaching Methods.* 4th ed. London: Kogan Page.

Davis, B. G. 1993. *Tools for Teaching.* San Francisco: Jossey-Bass.

Halpern, D. F., and associates. 1994. *Changing College Classrooms: New Teaching and Learning Strategies for an Increasingly Complex World.* San Francisco: Jossey-Bass.

Hedengren, B. F. 2004. *A TA's Guide to Teaching Writing in All Disciplines.* Boston: Bedford/St. Mark's.

McKeachie, W. J., and M. Svinicki. 2006. *McKeachie's Teaching Tips: Strategies, Research, and Theory for College and University Teachers.* 12th ed. Boston: Houghton Mifflin.

Meyers, C. 1993. *Promoting Active Learning: Strategies for the College Classroom.* San Francisco: Jossey-Bass.

Chapter 7
One-on-One Interaction with Students

Managing a classroom of many students is a complex task; equally important and challenging is working with individual students both inside and outside the classroom. This chapter offers suggestions to make your one-on-one dealings with students as effective, efficient, and comfortable as possible.

Office Hours

Most teaching assistants will hold one to three office hours each week. This time is usually provided so that students can drop in for individualized information, clarification, or advice.

Where to Hold Office Hours

Graduate programs typically provide office space to teaching assistants. Even when such an office is available, some teaching assistants prefer to meet with students in a public place, such as a coffee shop or a student lounge. We strongly recommend using a departmental office for office hours; the potential problems with meeting in a public place outweigh the potential benefits. Never meet at your home. Here are some of the pros and cons of each setting.

Meeting in a Departmental Office

PROS   It maintains your authority as a teacher and as a representative of the department for which you work.

It provides greater clarity about the nature of your meeting and your relationship with your students (specifically, you are the teacher).

It helps maintain appropriate boundaries between students and teachers; it is the blurring of these boundaries that encourages both students and teachers to think of each other as potential romantic objects. To this end, always keep the door to your office open; for discussions of a grade or other sensitive issues, you may want to close the door partway and lower your voice.

Meeting in the privacy of an office is a courtesy to students who come to your office hours to discuss sensitive issues such as their grades or personal problems that are affecting their work in the course.

Cons It can set up a more formal relationship than some teaching assistants would like to have with their students. However, the tone of your relationship with your students depends more on your approach and attitude than on the location of your meeting.

Departmental offices often lack "ambiance."

Meeting in a Coffee Shop

Pros Many graduate students do not like their offices (typically windowless cubbies). And if no students come to office hours, it can be more pleasant to spend two hours in a coffee shop than in a shoe box.

It may make students feel that you are more accessible to them than university professors can sometimes seem to students.

Cons It can blur boundaries and lead to misunderstandings about the nature of your relationship with your students.

Students may feel obligated to purchase a drink.

Students may have trouble finding you in a crowded coffee shop, or they may not have a suitable place to wait if you are already meeting with another student (or graduate student friend) when they get there.

There can be many distractions in coffee shops.

It is easy for other patrons to eavesdrop on your meeting, which is not fair to students who come to discuss sensitive issues such as their grades.

If your department does not provide you an office, try to find a public space on campus where students can easily find you and your conversations are not likely to be overheard (e.g., a public room in a library or student union).

Timing Office Hours

You will save yourself and your students a lot of trouble by holding office hours at times when the students probably will attend. In other words, while you may be able to get a lot of your own work done if you hold your office hours from 7:00 to 9:00 A.M., you will probably have to find other times during the week to meet with interested students. You may also want to consider making sure that your office hours are not at the same time each day. For example, if you hold office hours from 1:00 to 2:00 on Tuesdays and Thursdays, students who cannot come to the Tuesday time because of a class are likely to have the same class on Thursday. That said, also schedule your office hours such that they work well with your schedule and do not interrupt a long stretch of potential work time.

Naturally, you should be on time for your office hours and have all of the necessary course materials on hand. If you need to change your office hours, even for a week, notify your students in advance. If a student cannot attend your scheduled office hours, find another time when you both can meet.

Coordinating Student Meetings

How long you spend talking with one particular student will depend on the nature of their visit and how many other students are waiting to meet with you. If another student peers into your meeting, ask them to wait outside your office and tell them approximately how long the wait will be. After that period of time, tell the student in your office that to be fair, you need to meet with the student waiting outside the office.

Students Who Misuse Your Office Hours

You will occasionally come across students who are much better at making it to your office hours than they are at making it to your class. If a student starts coming to your office hours regularly to find out about what is going on in the section or the lecture (or both!), you will want to nip this behavior in the bud. The best approach is to inform the student kindly that you would be delighted to discuss and clarify any questions the student has about the section, lecture, or readings after the student has obtained class notes and reviewed all the material.

EXAMPLES   "Do you know anyone else in the class from whom you could get notes? Then if you have questions, we could talk about those specifically."

"Have you done the required reading for this week? Much of the material we talked about in class is covered there, so let's talk about what seemed unclear to you in the reading."

This is also a good time to remind the student about your attendance policy and the potential effect of multiple absences on their grade.

Ending Office Hours

If you are still meeting with a student when office hours end, feel free to state politely that your office hours are over. If necessary, offer to have the student return to your office hours next week to continue your discussion. Ending office hours can be difficult if you are in the middle of meeting with a student who is very upset or angry. Again, politely observe that your office hours have ended and that you can continue to talk with the student more in the future if necessary.

See "Students with Personal Problems" and "Grade Complaints" in this chapter for more information on how to end office hours.

E-mail

You should answer all e-mails from your students as quickly as possible, and you should send time-sensitive e-mails to students only if you know they check their e-mailboxes regularly. If a student sends you more e-mail than you can respond to electronically, suggest that the student come to your office hours so that you can answer a number of their questions at one time. A barrage of e-mails from a particular student can be the surface manifestation of a bigger issue (e.g., a student crush, excessive academic insecurity). Save all these e-mail messages and monitor the situation so that you can manage further developments, if they arise. Refer to the preceding section, "Students Who Misuse Your Office Hours," for information on how to address students who regularly e-mail you for information instead of coming to class.

E-mail Tone

You can set the tone when you use e-mail to communicate with your students. Some teaching assistants like to keep their e-mails formal, while other teaching assistants like to use e-mail as a forum for more casual course-related discussion. If you feel that a student's e-mails are overly familiar, all you have to do is bump up the formality of your response; most students will get the hint.

From a student:

Dear Sam,

I am in your Math 250 class. I was not in class on Wed. Sept 20th, due to the fact that I was suffering from a migraine headache. I was wondering if I could turn in my assignment for that day on Friday. If so I would really appreciate it. I do not have a doctor's note, but I do have prescribed medication that I can show you if it is necessary. My migraines bring me to the point of near stroke, thereby rendering me unfit to attend class. I will describe it in further detail if need be. Please write and let me know if I can turn in my assignment. I understand your attendance policy, and will accept a negative answer if you must give one. I look forward to hearing from you.

Your student, Peter

Your formal response:

Peter,

Thank you for the note explaining your absence. I will accept the assignment on Friday and will not mark it down, although the absence will have to count as one of the three absences you are allowed during the term. I hope you are feeling better, and I'll see you on Friday.

Sam

Your informal response:

Hi Peter. Thanks for the note. Your migraines sound miserable! I hope you are feeling recovered by this time—I hate to think of you teetering on the edge of stroke-dom. :-) Yes, I will accept your assignment on Friday, and I will give you full credit, given the nature of your absence. But I'm afraid that we'll have to count it as one of your three absences. Take care of that head, and I'll see you on Friday. —Sam

"Cc"-ing E-mail

If an e-mail conversation with a student becomes antagonistic or sensitive, or if you are discussing matters that may require departmental intervention, "cc" (i.e., send a copy to) the professor and/or the director of undergraduate studies in your response (and include the student's original message). This way, the professor or director of undergraduate studies can monitor the situation and understand the details of the interaction if you later need advice or intervention. It also automatically brings in a third party to defuse the personal nature of the interaction between you and your student. The presence of a "higher authority" may or may not alter the student's behavior, but it reminds them that your relationship is part of an institutional hierarchy.

E-mail Records

Save all of your e-mails from each of the courses that you teach for the duration of the semester (at least). This will provide you with an easily accessible record of your communications with students. Create a class file and save all class-related e-mail there, both messages from students and your responses (if you "cc" yourself in your response, you will be more likely to remember to save it).

Students with Attendance Problems

Some college students feel they no longer should have to abide by attendance or lateness policies. If you have a formal attendance policy, spell out explicitly on the syllabus how many absences students are allowed and how students' grades will be affected by additional absences. Also tell students the point in time (e.g., twenty minutes) at which "lateness" becomes an absence (otherwise students may come to the last ten minutes of class to avoid an absence). Then, be consistent in enforcing the policy, or else some students may exploit your leniency.

Handling Student Excuses

Once students have used their allowed number of absences, they often will come to you with a distressing or complicated story about their next absence. Their story may well be true, but that does not necessarily make it an excused absence. Sympathize with their predicament but firmly explain that if it were not for their previous absences, this absence would not be a problem. Allowed absences are not meant as days when students can skip class; you provide them knowing that emergencies can arise during the semester and students may have to miss class. If your students do not need them, they should not use these allowed absences.

Handling Excessive Student Absence

Students will usually miss multiple classes for two reasons: (1) they don't care about the class; (2) something has gone very wrong in their personal lives. The first case is often grounds for failure, especially if students also are not handing in work. Do not feel guilty about this— these students know they deserve to fail for such behavior.

Students who miss many classes for personal reasons, unfortunately, still may have missed too many classes to do well or perhaps even to pass the course. If they won't be able to attend all future classes and make up missed work, you can offer to give them a withdrawal from the class or an incomplete rather than failing them. It is your responsibility as an instructor not to pass students who do not complete the work in the course for whatever reason, but you usually have the option to authorize the student's withdrawal from the course rather than fail them. Again, you will want to diagnose this problem before deciding on a solution.

See "Students with Personal Problems" in this chapter for more information on how to handle this situation.

Students with Learning Disabilities

The Nature of Learning Disabilities

Universities and their students are increasingly aware that there are competent students who also have learning disabilities. There is no relationship between being intelligent and having a learning disability; students with learning disabilities simply have some specific difficulty receiving or communicating information in one or more of the ways that are most common in academic settings.

What the Student Should Do

It is up to the student to alert you to their learning disability and tell you what kind of special accommodations they need before the first assignments are due or the first exam is administered. Students should come to you at the beginning of the term with official documentation of the problem and a request for special assistance. Any student with a learning disability should be able to provide a letter from the appropriate university office. This documentation likely will specify what you should do as an instructor and ensure that privileges associated with learning disabilities are not abused.

What the Teaching Assistant Should Do

Put a note on your syllabus asking students with learning disabilities or other special needs that you will need to accommodate to notify you immediately. When a student comes to you about a learning disability, you should make every effort to accommodate their special needs. However, you are not under any obligation to provide retroactive help to a student who alerts you to their learning disability after they already have had trouble in your class. Ask them what special accommodations they need for the next assignment or exam and encourage them to tell their other instructors about the learning disability as soon as possible.

If you feel that a student's requests for special accommodations are unreasonable, contact the university office that issued the official documentation for advice on what is considered appropriate.

Student: I want to talk to you about my grade on the last exam. I didn't do very well, and part of the problem is that I have a learning disability that makes it hard for me to work under time pressure.

TA: I am glad you let me know that you have a learning disability that got in the way of your performance on the exam. If this is causing you such serious problems, you should get documentation from the student services office that specifies the kinds of accommodations you need. Then we can arrange what you need for the next exam. In the future, you should let your instructors know about your disability at the beginning of the semester so that you get the support you need for the whole semester.

Student: Well, it works for me to take the same exam as everyone else but to just have more time to do it. But I am also worried that this bad first exam will hurt my grade in the course.

> TA: Okay, if you can get me the documentation of the learning dis-
> ability, it should be no problem to arrange for you to get extra
> time. As for the last exam, it would not be fair to the other stu-
> dents to let you retake the exam, even with your disability. This is
> why it is important that you let your instructors know about your
> disability at the beginning of the semester rather than waiting until
> you get a disappointing grade.

Students with Personal Problems

The Nature of Personal Problems

There are students with personal problems, and these problems often
affect their academic performance. College students are at least as likely
to suffer from troubles such as depression, eating disorders, drug or
alcohol abuse, and violent relationships as are people in the "real
world." You may become aware of a student's personal problems in a
number of ways. Sometimes, a student will identify you as a caring person in a position of authority and come to you directly, send you an e-
mail, or attach a note to an assignment to alert you to the problem.
Other times, you will become aware of a student's personal problem
when it interferes with the student's ability to do their work in your
course.

What the Teaching Assistant Should Do

It is not your job to diagnose or treat the problem. While you will want
to be supportive of your students, you will compromise your role as a
teacher if you also try to be a therapist. Do not try to solve the student's
problem. What you *can* do is help the student become aware of how
their problem is interfering with their performance in your class (if they
are not already aware of it) and point them toward help. Many university campuses offer free mental health services and academic counseling
to students. It is highly likely that at some point you will come across a
student who needs some sort of counseling; make a point of finding out
about what services are available at your university.

It is a very natural reaction to want to accommodate the student as
much as possible, especially if they seem upset, penitent, or frantic. But
you may not be doing them a favor if you excuse them from the responsibilities of the class. If their problem is such that they cannot handle

their academic workload, they must confront this situation and seek outside help. They may need counseling or time off from school. Think of it as a "strict parent policy" in which you are enforcing fair rules and teaching students how to fulfill their responsibilities. Additionally, you can express your understanding that there are some semesters when difficult life events take priority over schoolwork. What is critical is that the student meet the problem head-on so that they can prioritize school again as soon as possible.

Talking with the Student

A student's personal problems often will be quite severe before they significantly affect academic performance. You should not approach a student about a personal problem unless you are quite sure that something is going wrong for that student outside of the classroom. While you may be able to speculate about what is going wrong, you will have the most effective conversation with a student if you focus on what you do know: how the student is doing in your class. For example, you may notice that a student misses class often and smells of alcohol when they do come. Or, a student may seem to be extremely "down" and ask for repeated extensions on papers because they are unable to work productively.

Where and When to Talk with Students about Personal Problems

If you need to talk with a student about the ways a personal problem is affecting their work in the class, be sure to do it at a time and place where the student is likely to feel comfortable and where the conversation will not be overheard. Your departmental office may be a good place for a meeting like this. If you do not have a planned conference with the student, you will need to make a time to meet with them. If you need to plan a meeting, ask the student to stay after class and then make sure that you get them to set up a meeting with you.

TA:	Jamie, I want to talk with you about your work for the class. Could you meet with me on Wednesday at 4:00?
Student:	No, I have practice then.
TA:	O.K., when are some times next week that would work for you to meet?

What to Say in the Meeting

Regardless of what is going wrong for the student, once you have arranged a meeting, you can talk with your student about their work and suggest extra help in the following manner.

EXAMPLE   "Jamie, I've noticed that you are missing class a lot lately and that you failed the most recent exam after getting a B+ on the first one. It seems like things outside of class may be making it hard for you to do your best in here. If you are interested, there are support services around campus, such as the counseling center, which can help you relieve stresses that are getting in the way of your academic work. I wanted to talk with you to find ways for you to do the best work you can in the course right now."

Keep your focus on the student's performance in the class. You and the student must determine if and how they can improve their performance in the class and how you can assist in *that* process.

When a Student "Blows You Off"

It is the student's prerogative not to take your advice. In this case, be sure that you are clear with the student about where they stand academically and then do not pursue the issue further. Do not consider your efforts wasted: some people will seek out much-needed counseling only after they have heard the suggestion from a variety of people.

When a Student Approaches You

More commonly, a student will come to you to discuss a personal problem. When this happens, be sensitive to what they are telling you, without letting them "spill" too much. If you allow a student to give you an overly detailed account of their personal problem (e.g., confusion about how to handle their girlfriend's pregnancy), you risk blurring the boundary between being their teacher and being their friend or counselor. As soon as feels comfortable, you can use the following guidelines to respond to the student.

• Acknowledge the problem and be sympathetic.

EXAMPLE   "You were right to let me know that this has been going on
           for you, and it sounds really stressful. It is not uncommon
           for people to have trouble with (depression/eating disor-
           ders/romantic or family relationships)."

- If it feels like an appropriate time, tell the student about the university services available to help them with their problem.

EXAMPLE   "Sometimes, it can really help to talk with someone about
           this kind of problem. If you are feeling like it would help to
           talk to someone besides your family and friends, you could
           contact the university counseling center, which has services
           available to students for just this sort of situation."

- Talk with the student about where they stand in your class and how
  you can work together to get them caught up on the work. If the
  student's mood makes it impossible to have a productive conversation, arrange for a future meeting.

When a Student Cannot Do the Work

Sometimes a student's problems will become so overwhelming that they
stop attending class or cannot do the required work. You must step in at
this point and alert the student that they cannot pass the course given this
situation. If you feel the student's problems justify it, you can offer to
withdraw them from the course rather than failing them. Do not feel
guilty about this kind of action. These students know that they are inca-
pable of doing the work, and they are rarely surprised by such consequences. While you may feel tempted to bend over backward to help the
student through your class, this behavior may not be as helpful as you
think it is. Many people will get help for severe personal problems only
when they are faced with a clear consequence related to the problem, such
as having to withdraw from a class. Be firm but also remember that it is
important to express sympathy within appropriate boundaries; authority
figures who are not appropriately sympathetic can be very hurtful.

Antagonistic Students

You will have antagonistic students. At times, students will make comments or write papers that are more antagonistic than thoughtful.

Though some students will do this by design, others will not even be aware they are being offensive or antagonistic. Your first reaction may be to protect yourself or other students from potential harm caused by an antagonistic student's words. But your role as a teacher allows you to deal with these circumstances in a way that is constructive, not simply defensive. You want to promote intellectual disagreement; it is critical to a serious and productive learning environment. It is your job to help students present arguments and counterarguments that can be taken seriously.

See chapter 4, "Disruptive Students: The Antagonistic Debater," for more information on how to handle this behavior in class.

Problematic Terminology

Sometimes students will unknowingly use terms or phrases that are offensive to you or to their fellow students. Sometimes students will knowingly use offensive terminology in order to antagonize you or their fellow students. First you'll need to make a diagnosis: is the offense intentional or not?

If the student is using offensive language unwittingly, it usually only takes one comment (spoken or written) to remedy this situation. Gently explain to the student that there are more accepted terms and that they should be aware of the connotations of the terms they are presently using.

If the student is being deliberately offensive, you still need to see this as a teachable moment, both for the student and for their classmates. It is your responsibility to ensure that your classroom is a comfortable and productive learning environment. You can take this opportunity to talk with students about the wider ramifications of this kind of language and its power to derail any discourse, including a classroom discussion. Assuming that the student has a valid point to make, you can also show the student how this phrasing serves only to undermine the effectiveness of their argument.

See chapter 4, "Disruptive Students: The Bomb Dropper," for more information on how to handle this behavior in class.

> "I had a first-year student who used the word *queer* to refer to things he thought were weird. I pulled him aside two weeks into class and gently explained to him how and why that word might be offensive to his classmates. He was shocked: the term was used at his high school all the time, and he had no idea it could be offensive."

Problematic Arguments

At times, students will mistake polemic for proof. This is especially likely when students have strong personal and antagonistic feelings about an issue. Your best approach is to show students how weak a proofless polemic is. Push students (either in spoken discussion or in written comments) to defend their positions with specific facts and a recognition of the merits of their argument in light of opposing views. Antagonistic arguments are often based on generalizations and empty rhetoric. When grading papers with these kinds of arguments you can show students (with your comments and their grade) that this kind of argument—antagonistic or not—is not effective. If your grading is based on the quality of the argument, you can explain it to the student without having to engage in a personal discussion of your views on this particular issue.

When Reason Fails

In extreme cases, you may find that talking with an antagonistic student or writing reasonable comments on their papers is failing to curb their behavior. You can begin by consulting with the professor or with the director of undergraduate studies about how to control the student's behavior in class or how to respond effectively to their written assignments. Make and keep copies of the student's antagonistic writing if you feel that you may need to seek advice from other teachers. If any part of your interaction with this student is occurring on e-mail, "cc" (i.e., send a copy to) the professor and/or the director of undergraduate studies to keep them informed on how the situation is progressing. The director of undergraduate studies has the authority and responsibility to meet with students if their behavior becomes disruptive and to transfer them to another section if necessary.

These situations can prove to be personally upsetting. Use the professor and your colleagues as moral support so that you are not drawn into a personal debate with the student. You will never gain by letting yourself become visibly angry or irrational with the student, so find other outlets for your frustration, hurt, or anger.

"Once I had a student who wrote a paper entitled 'Democrats Suck.' He had clearly written it to antagonize me, to see what I would do. I gave him a D. I gave him that grade not because I disagreed with him but because the paper was terribly written. He immediately e-mailed me to ask for a conference about the grade. I knew it was going to be an unpleasant conference, and beforehand, I went over all the problems in the argument and in the proof so that I felt prepared. When I met with him, I was open about our differences in political views, and I acknowledged that some of his criticisms of liberals were potentially strong points. I then pointed out all the structural weaknesses in the paper itself. I pushed him for specifics to back up his generalizations and pointed out his leaps in logic. He walked away angry, but more with writing than with me."

Fraternizing with Students

Social Activities with Students

Though you may like many of your students, it is not appropriate to include them in your social circle while you are their instructor. Socializing with your students can compromise your professional authority. Students are not necessarily prepared to think of you both as a peer and as an authority figure; it is critical that you not compromise the latter in an effort to "connect" with your students. In addition, socializing with your students exposes you to all sorts of risks.

- Many students drink illegally; you do not want to be a part of this activity, even as a witness.

- Spending time with your students as a peer encourages them to think of you as a potential romantic interest.

- Spending time with your students as a peer encourages them to think they can ask you favors about grades, exams, or other course work as a friend.

- Here is a scenario to avoid: a student blithely mentions to their parents that they were out drinking with their teaching assistant on Friday night. The parents call your department to ask about the appropriateness of that behavior.

You have lots of people who can be your friends. Let your students be your students. So, if you are invited to come to a student party or to join your students for a drink after class, thank them for the invitation and tell them that you cannot make it.

Socializing with former students, once the term is over, can still be problematic. They or their friends may take classes from you in the future, and appropriate teacher-student boundaries may be more difficult to maintain. However, one potentially rewarding part of teaching is maintaining ongoing mentoring relationships with some students. Use your judgment in establishing such relationships.

Crushes

Crushes can go both ways. However, it is more common for students to develop crushes on their teaching assistants. These crushes often are harmless, as both the student and the instructor know that the student has no plans to pursue this romantic possibility. Ignore these crushes unless the student decides to act on their feelings. Be firm in turning down invitations for social activities and, if necessary, tell the student explicitly that romantic relationships between students and instructors are not appropriate.

> *Student:* I was wondering if you would want to grab coffee with me some-time.
>
> *TA:* If you would like to talk about the course, I would be happy to talk with you during my office hours or to make another appointment if that time doesn't work.
>
> *Student:* No, I was just wanting to grab coffee and hang out.
>
> *TA:* I appreciate the offer, but I find that it doesn't work for teaching assistants and students to hang out together socially.
>
> *Student:* Right, but I was thinking that we could just get to know each other better.
>
> *TA:* Well, thank you for asking, but like I said, it won't work.
>
> *Student:* Well, how about when the semester's over?
>
> *TA:* I really don't think that will be feasible.

Teaching assistants also can find particular students attractive. Do not act upon this attraction and be careful not to show any favoritism toward a student you find attractive. Do not allow yourself to consider the possibility of a romantic relationship with a student, even as something to be discussed as a "future possibility." Do not dabble in the gray areas (e.g., inviting a student "just" for coffee); most students will feel obliged to accept such an invitation even if they would rather not—a situation that could feel to a student like sexual harassment.

Once the term is over, you are technically free to do as you please at most schools, taking into account that your responsibilities as an instructor can extend beyond the term (requests for recommendations, enrollment in another course with you). But during the term, you should in no way jeopardize your teacher-student relationship.

Attraction between students and teaching assistants is a tricky area. You must not forget that the power dynamic of the classroom affects *all* of your relationships with students, including ones that feel like genuine attraction. The difference between romance and sexual harassment is that sexual harassment involves a power differential that could potentially be abused.

See the next section, "Sexual Harassment," for more information about what constitutes harassment.

> "The second time I taught first-year composition, I had sixteen first-year men in the class, about ten of whom stared at me with adoring, puppy-dog eyes during every class meeting. And they would come to my office hours all the time. 'I have an idea for my paper—can I come talk to you about it?' 'Will you take a look at my rough draft?' 'Will you read my new introduction?' But it was all very safe (and very endearing). I knew they weren't going to do anything about these crushes, and they knew they weren't going to do anything either. And, whatever their motives, their writing sure did get a lot better!"

Sexual Harassment

Sexual harassment involves an abuse of power. Teachers always have more institutional power than students; students sometimes have more physical or cultural power than teachers. Sexual harassment between teachers and students can go both ways. Instructors may be sexually harassed by a student, but it usually happens the other way around.

Sexual Harassment by Teaching Assistants

You are in the position of authority with regard to your students; you must, therefore, be especially careful not to abuse your power. Many teaching assistants are close enough in age to their students that they may flirt with the idea of having a romantic encounter with one of them. These thoughts may be fueled by the fact that students often have crushes on their teaching assistants. Under no circumstances should you pursue a romantic and/or sexual relationship with a current student. In addition, you should never do *anything* that might be construed by a reasonable person as a sexual advance.

DON'T Touch your students.

Make suggestive comments to them.

Use "racy" or sexually explicit language inappropriately in class.

Ask students to read "racy" or explicit material aloud in class or to write sexually explicit or provocative papers.

Invite a student for a "datelike" encounter (e.g., coffee, lunch, a movie).

Encourage a student to call you at home.

Call a student at home unless absolutely necessary for class-related business; whenever possible, use e-mail.

Meet with a student at your home—or theirs—even about strictly academic matters.

Meet with a student behind closed doors. If a student has come to you about a personal problem, lowered voices can provide the necessary privacy. See "Students with Personal Problems" in this chapter for more information on how to handle this situation.

Discuss your personal life with your students.

These guidelines hold for students of the opposite sex or of the same sex. It is a mistake to think that sexual harassment occurs only across sexes.

While these guidelines are designed to protect your students, they also protect you. At the most basic level, you do not want to do anything that would expose you to an accusation of sexual harassment. More generally, you do not want to compromise your position as an educator or your students' ability to feel comfortable learning in your classroom.

Sexual Harassment by Students

Defining Sexual Harassment by Students

The standards for what constitutes sexual harassment by a student are slightly different than those for harassment by an instructor. Without the power differential to abuse, harassment in this case is defined as any action that continues after an explicit "no." Anything that feels like sexual harassment needs to be stopped as quickly as possible. Sexual harassment by a student can include (but is not limited to) the following.

EXAMPLES   A student makes subtle sexual comments to you after you have told them this is inappropriate.

A student asks you out for a date again after you definitively have said "no" the first time.

A student says grossly inappropriate things to you after you have told them what they are doing is inappropriate.

A student tries to touch you in a sexual way.

Responding to Sexual Harassment by Students

Your response needs to be firm and authoritative. If any part of this kind of interaction occurs on e-mail, send a copy of your responses to the director of undergraduate studies (including the student's original message) to defuse the personal nature of the conversation and to alert the director to a potentially problematic situation.

EXAMPLES   If the student says things to you that make you uncomfortable, you may tell the student that their comments are inappropriate and leave it at that. If the student continues this behavior, you can tell them that you will be forced to report them because this kind of behavior constitutes harassment.

If you are asked on a date, you can say that it is not appropriate for teaching assistants to date their students. Saying, "I'm sorry, I'm busy" is not a definitive "no."

If the student makes grossly inappropriate comments after you have told them to stop or tries to touch you in a sexual way, you have a choice to make: you can report the behavior to the proper campus authorities immediately, or you can tell the student that their behavior is not acceptable and that you will report it to the campus authorities if it happens again.

These situations are uncomfortable and unpleasant. Do not let your discomfort prevent you from responding with clarity and authority.

Most universities have an office that handles issues of sexual harassment. You should feel free to consult this office, the professor for the course, or the director of undergraduate studies for advice and moral support, even if you are uncertain about whether you will file a formal complaint.

Plagiarism

Find out about your university's policy on plagiarism and explain this to students (in all seriousness) early in the term. If students will write papers for the course, carefully review how outside information (quotations and ideas) must be cited. Leave no room for questions about what constitutes plagiarism or the repercussions for doing it. Explain to your students that they may have their own questions about the proper citation of sources and that they should feel free to look to you for answers.

Minimizing Opportunities for Plagiarism

The best way to avoid plagiarism is to design assignments so specific to your course that students will not be able to copy material. Alternatively, or in addition, ask to see drafts of an assignment or have students discuss preliminary ideas with you (it is very hard to plagiarize a rough draft).

In addition, tell your students that you know about the term papers that are available in most fraternities and sororities and that you are familiar with the term-paper web sites (even if you aren't!). If students know that you are clued in to these resources, they will be less likely to risk using them.

Helping Students Use the Internet Appropriately

With the growing popularity of the Internet, many students will do a preliminary Internet search on a topic before embarking on a paper or project. The Internet can be a valuable research tool if students know how to use it as such; you should explain to students the scholarly value of different types of Internet sites in your field and how they can begin to identify and use them. The Internet is also challenging traditional notions of copyright and plagiarism. Review with students how to cite information found on the Internet, whether it be general ideas or specific quotations.

Spotting Plagiarism

There are often fairly clear signals of plagiarism.

- The topic of the paper is only marginally related to the assignment.
- The tone or style of the paper is noticeably different from the student's previous work.
- The paper contains statistics, references, or facts that are not readily accessible to the student.
- There are very few grammatical mistakes or even awkward sentences.
- Two students hand in papers that are strikingly similar in the presentation and sequence of ideas.

Students sometimes will intersperse their own sentences or paragraphs into the plagiarized text, and you will notice shifts in style, tone, and grammatical correctness among these sections.

Unfortunately, you must accept that you will miss a certain amount of plagiarism. There are term papers on file in most fraternities and sororities, and there are now web sites of term papers on the Internet. Because these resources are widely available, you are best off tailoring assignments to make most of these "model papers" useless for your students.

EXAMPLES   Find a magazine advertisement that you think is interesting. Describe the techniques it employs to sell the product. Attach the advertisement to the paper when you hand it in.

Imagine that you are writing the introduction to a volume of articles that includes the articles by Sanchez and Miller that we have read. In 500 words, explain to readers how the articles' arguments intersect.

Checking for Plagiarism

If you suspect a paper has been plagiarized, you have a few relatively quick options to check to see whether you can find the true source.

- Do a Lexis/Nexis or ProQuest search on the topic to find any relevant news articles that the student might have used.

- Search academic indexes for relevant scholarly articles.

- Do an Internet search on the topic.

- Type a suspicious phrase or sentence (surrounded by quotation marks) into Google.

There is a good chance, however, that you will not be able to identify the source; do not waste much of your time in this pursuit.

Meeting with Your Professor

Before you talk with the student about the paper, you should alert the professor that there may be a problem and decide on a course of action. You can draw on the professor's experience with these matters. And you want to make sure that you and the professor agree on how the matter should be handled.

> "One semester I caught two students turning in virtually the same paper. Plagiarism doesn't get much more obvious than that! I told both students that they would be failed for the paper and might be referred to the board for academic discipline. But when I told the professor what I had done, he said, 'Oh no, in a case like this, I simply ask the students to rewrite the papers.' So, I then had to go back to the students and report the professor's decision. Needless to say, I felt like my authority as their teacher was shot for the rest of the semester."

Using University Resources

Most colleges and universities have offices that handle academic misconduct by students. You should feel free to consult with them at any point in the process as you decide upon a course of action. You may also want or need to forward the case to that office, after talking with the student, for a final determination on the case and for any sanctions at the university level (e.g., academic probation). University administrators ask instructors to alert their office about a student's academic misconduct so that they can determine whether this is a one-time offense or part of a larger pattern.

Tempering Your Reaction

If you think or know that a student has plagiarized a paper, it is easy to feel angry and offended. But initially you must give the student the benefit of the doubt and allow them to explain if they can. Even if you have thoroughly discussed plagiarism in class, some students will not understand that, for example, rephrasing material from a source without citing it constitutes plagiarism. Or they will quote parts of a text and copy other parts of the same text without realizing that their citations do not cover the unquoted material.

Therefore, see your first job as "investigating the nature of the crime" to determine the circumstances and intentions. Start by saying, "I was wondering where you got this information." The student may innocently tell you the source, and then you can discuss appropriate citation of secondary material. If the student claims the work is their own and you know it is not, then you have a clear case of plagiarism.

Talking with the Student

You should always talk with the student about a plagiarized or suspicious paper. The student should have the opportunity to explain what happened before any further action is taken. You can e-mail the student before you return papers and say that you need to set up a meeting to talk about the paper. Or when you return papers, you can tell the student that you need to meet with them individually to talk about the paper before you can grade it.

A Clear Case of Plagiarism

If you have the source of a plagiarized paper, we encourage you not to play games with the student by asking them how they came up with the idea. You can simply show the student the source and their paper and say, "Please explain to me how this happened."

An Unclear Case of Plagiarism

If you strongly suspect plagiarism, start the conversation by telling the student that, after reading the paper, you realized that you need to speak with them before you could grade it. There are then several ways to proceed.

Ask the student to tell you more about a confusing or interesting idea in the paper; this will quickly reveal the student's grasp of the material.

- Ask the student why they chose to write on this topic—and feel free to push them hard for a reason.

- Point to a passage that does not sound like their writing and ask them about the shift in tone or style.

- Ask the student to talk more about a source they cite in the paper.

Your suspicions will quickly become clear to the student, and that is unavoidable. Sometimes it will also quickly become clear that the student cannot talk knowledgeably about the paper. In this case, stop the conversation and simply ask, "Explain to me why you cannot talk about your paper." Sometimes the student will be able to talk knowledgeably about the paper, in which case you may not have any solid grounds for suspecting plagiarism.

The Dynamics of the Conversation

When students are pushed and realize that they have been "found out," they will sometimes admit guilt and plead extenuating circumstances. Students may also beg you to handle the case "in house" rather than alerting the professor or university office. The student will often frame the situation as if you had a choice about how to proceed. You should remind the student that they have put you in a position in which you must alert particular administrators about their academic misconduct.

EXAMPLE   "I appreciate your honesty, and I too am sorry that we're having to have this conversation. But plagiarism is serious and needs to be dealt with at the departmental and university level."

At the end of all conversations about plagiarism, you do not need to have the answer ready about what will happen next; often you will find that you need time to think about the situation and talk with the professor or director of undergraduate studies. You can say to the student that the conversation has helped you to understand more about the situation and that you will get back to them about what will happen next.

If the student becomes belligerent or offended and does not admit to any wrongdoing, yet you still believe after the conversation that the student has not written all of the material in the paper, you should end the conversation. There is little to gain by arguing with the student; you will need to bring in a third party, whether that is the professor, the director of undergraduate studies, or a university administrator.

EXAMPLE   "It seems that we see this situation differently. Let's stop
           for now so that I can consult with Professor Marshall, and
           I'll get back to you about what will happen next."

The Follow-up to the Conversation

After your conversation with the student, you (and the professor, if appropriate) will have a choice to make. You may decide to turn the matter over to the appropriate university office for a decision and possible action. You do not need to be certain about the suspected plagiarism case to do this; you only need to have a strong suspicion of wrongdoing. A student who is found to have committed academic misconduct by this office will likely face consequences at the university level (e.g., academic probation). You must then work with the course professor to determine appropriate consequences for the student in your course (e.g., failing the paper, failing the course).

If the student's protests have left you with serious doubts about whether plagiarism occurred, you may decide to deal with the matter yourself. Again, talk with the professor teaching the course to decide how to proceed. For example, the student can be asked to redo the assignment, to do the same assignment with better citations, and so forth. In some cases, you will simply have to swallow your suspicions and grade the paper. At some point, it is not a good use of your time to try to track down sources of papers you suspect are plagiarized.

In both clear and suspected cases of plagiarism, keep copies of all the student's work in case you are faced with another suspected violation of academic codes of conduct by the same student later in the term.

Enforcing Plagiarism Policies

If the plagiarism is the result of honest ignorance (e.g., if the student rephrased sentences without citing the source as opposed to copying entire paragraphs or an entire paper), you can see your meeting with them as a warning and as an important part of the student's education. Admonish them about the seriousness of plagiarism and alert them to the fact that they probably will not see such leniency again in their academic career. Have the student rewrite the paper and then grade it.

If it is a case of blatant plagiarism and you have identified the source or the student has confessed, consult with the professor for the course or the director of undergraduate studies and then follow the university's policy for handling this offense. There are no extenuating circumstances that make plagiarism acceptable. Because plagiarism is arguably the gravest offense at a university, it is critical that you take it seriously. Allow the university board for academic discipline to handle the matter.

Cheating

Cheating often is not hard to catch if you are alert and watch for it during an exam.

Proctoring Exams

There are easy steps to take to minimize the opportunities for cheating.

- Have students move their desks apart (if the desks are movable).

- Have students sit in every other seat in a lecture hall with fixed chairs.

- Make students put all papers, books, and cell phones into their bags and close them.

- Walk around the room during the exam period, and if you are sitting in the front, look up often.

- If any students are acting suspicious, watch them carefully (do not be subtle about this) or stand near them.

- Ask students wearing baseball caps to take them off or wear them bill backward so that you can see where their eyes are looking.

- Have two forms of the same exam—the forms can have the same questions but in a different order.

Catching Cheating

If you are proctoring an exam and catch a student using a "cheat sheet" (or a "cheat cap" or a "cheat arm"), *quietly* confiscate the illegal material (if possible!). Ask the student where they are in the exam and mark that spot. Say to the student, "Finish the exam. I will discuss this with you when I grade the exams." If it is not possible to confiscate the material (without the amputation of a limb), take the student's exam and ask them to sit quietly until everyone else is finished in order to avoid a disturbance.

When you are grading the exams, consult with the professor and decide on a course of action. Inform the student of your decision; if you are concerned that the student will be belligerent, ask the professor to attend the meeting.

Grading Exams

If you find exams with strikingly similar answers and/or mistakes, you must talk with the students involved. First, tell the professor about the problem if you are leading a discussion section of a larger lecture and ask the professor to attend your meetings with the students. Meet with the students individually. Tell each one that you have found unusual similarities between their exam and another student's and ask them to explain.

Grade Complaints

You can be fairly certain that, at some point along the line (and probably sooner rather than later), you will get a complaint about a paper, an exam, a quiz, or a final grade. There are a few universal reasons for grade complaints.

- Some first-year students who did well in high school may be shocked by their first set of (lower) college grades, and you may bear the brunt of that adjustment period.

- Some students will try to contest a grade just to see if you will change it; they may not believe they deserve a better grade, but they would be more than happy to get one anyway. They think it is at least worth a try.

- Some students will think that they can flirt a teaching assistant into giving them a better grade.

- Some male students will think that they can intimidate a female teaching assistant into giving them a better grade.

- You gave a particularly hard assignment or exam, and many students struggled.

- You give lower grades than another teaching assistant students have had.

Keep an open mind when discussing the grade but do not assume that you are wrong. The fact that a student has taken the time to come to office hours to question a grade does not justify a grade change. But naturally, if the error is yours, be gracious about changing the grade. Doing so in no way undermines your authority; stubbornly refusing to recognize a mistake does.

Complaints about a Graded Assignment

When you return graded material, be sure to tell students how the material was graded as well as when and how they should contact you with questions or concerns. If the majority of the grades were low and you expect students may be upset, do not hesitate to tell the class where they had problems and how they can deal with this grade in order to get a better final grade. Always remember that the final grade is a focal point for them and you are not "coming down a level" to discuss what they need to do in order to get the grade they want; see it instead as an incentive that makes them work harder.

When a student comes to your office hours with a grade complaint, discuss the grade with them calmly and rationally (regardless of their attitude). Do your best to be fair, poised, and authoritative in these situations. Indeed, the most difficult aspect of grade complaints is that students may take their grades very personally and may try to engage you in a discussion about what you have "done" to them. Never meet this approach head-on. Immediately shift the conversation away from being about a problem between you and the student. The grade reflects the student's mastery of the material; position yourself as the helpful and informative teacher who is interested in helping the student increase their understanding of the course material.

Regardless of how the student approaches you, treat their grade complaint as a welcomed opportunity to clarify any confusion the student has about how you did your grading, the scoring system in the class, or the course material itself.

Don't   Immediately jump to the defensive and feel you must list every problem in the graded assignment.

Discuss grades right after class; students need time to digest the grade or your comments (and perhaps write a response).

Do   Ask the student to come to the meeting with a written paragraph explaining what grade they feel would be appropriate for the work so that you can use it as a basis for discussion.

Make the student do most of the talking in a grade complaint situation.

Listen for where the student might have misunderstood the material and offer clarification.

At the beginning of the meeting, ask the student to explain what in your comments they did not understand and why they believe the grade is not appropriate.

Pick out the major problems you addressed in your written comments and ask the student to talk through their response to these criticisms.

Put their grade in the context of the other grades in the class; they may need a reminder that grades are relative and that other students may be doing better work.

Refer them to the criteria you established in the beginning of the course about grades; the clearer the criteria, the easier this situation is to handle.

See chapter 8, "Grading Papers," for more on grading criteria.

A Complaint about an Essay Grade

Student: I don't understand why I got a C on this paper. I worked really hard on it.

TA: I know you worked hard on it. Did you understand my comments on the paper?

Student: (looking at the comments): Well, yeah. But I don't see why they make it a C paper. I know the organization could have been a little better, but you said the ideas were all okay.

TA: So if you were going to revise this paper, how would you reorganize it?

Student: (Muddles their way through trying to reorganize their ideas.)

TA: That sounds much better. But as you can see, those are some pretty drastic changes you're going to have to make to clarify your argument. And if you remember on the grading criteria handout, I told you that a B paper can only have minor lapses in organization. Now, did you understand what parts of the paper I was referring to when I wrote that you needed to expand some of these ideas? (And so on.)

A Complaint about an Exam Score

Student: I think you took off too many points on my exam. Why did I lose half the points on question 6?

TA: You only answered half the question. You needed to provide an explanation for why the mutation happens.

Student: But the question is really confusing and it doesn't really say you have to explain it.

TA: It is a long question, but it does ask you to provide an explanation. Other students in the class did, so it is only fair to give them credit for having done so.

A Complaint about Consistently Poor Grades

Student: You keep giving me bad grades on my papers. And I keep doing what you say, and then you give me another bad grade.

TA: I understand how frustrating this is. In part it's because my expectations go up with each paper. You need to fix the problems I comment on, but you also need to push yourself a step farther.

Student: But I don't think I'll ever get more than a B.

TA: You are very capable of getting a higher grade, but you're really going to have to push yourself to do it. If you remember on the grade-explanation criteria handout, I wrote that an A paper shows innovation or pushes boundaries in some way. That is hard to do, and it involves more than just fixing mechanics.

A Complaint about "Hard Grading"

Student: You graded this test way too hard. My roommate took this course last year and said that if I studied, I would do well. And I studied, and you gave me a C+.

TA: I graded the exam as fairly as possible, and there was a wide range of grades in the class. Some students did very well. Remember, your grade is not a reward for hard work. It's a measure of your mastery of the material.

A Belligerent Complaint

Student: I was really surprised to get my final grade for the course. I got a B– when I was expecting an A–.

TA: Here's how I computed your final grade: you got a B on the first paper and a C on the second and third paper. I have you down for an A on the final exam and a B for class participation and attendance.

Student: Why did I get a B for class participation? I talked every day!

TA: You did participate on the days that you were there, but you also had four absences. I outlined clearly in the syllabus that your participation grade would be lowered for every absence past your second.

Student: That's not fair! I had to go to my grandmother's funeral. Did you expect me to miss that for your stupid class?!

TA: Of course not. Unfortunately you already had three other absences when you had to go to her funeral.

Student: I can't believe this, I worked really hard in this class, and you stuck me with a B–, which is now part of my permanent record.

TA: I know that it is disappointing to get a lower grade than you expected, but I graded you and everyone else according to the standards that I set out at the beginning of the semester. I would be happy to adjust your grade if you found that I had miscalculated your points on any assignment or your total points for the semester. Otherwise, your grade stands as it is.

Student: This is unbelievable. You've totally screwed up my transcript, and you won't do anything about it!

TA: Like I said, you will need to show me where I graded you unfairly. Short of that, I cannot change your grade. I'm afraid we're going to have to stop this discussion for today. If you would like to, you can choose to talk with Professor Barry or to meet with the director of undergraduate studies.

Student: That's it?! That's all you'll do?!

TA: Yes, that is all I will do. I have other students to meet with now.

Student storms out of office, muttering obscenities under her breath.

TA, clearly shaken, reassures himself that it is more important to be fair to all of his students than it is to adjust his standard for belligerent students.

Complaints about a Final Grade

Make the student do most of the talking in a conference about a final grade. Remind them that unless you have made a mathematical error in calculating their grade, it is not fair to change their grade and not their classmates' grades. Some students might argue that they need a B+ instead of a B to get into the graduate school of their choice and believe that you can and will change the grade for them. Emphasize to them how unfair this action would be for all the other students in the class.

Some students will ask about their grade on e-mail. Here is an effective formula to follow in your response.

Marvin,

I appreciate your concern about the grade, and I am glad that you asked for clarification. According to my records, you got a B– on the midterm, a B on the final, a C and a B+ on the two papers, and a B+ on the presentation. You were absent four times, and as you were only allowed three absences, that affected your participation grade. Following the grade percentages on the syllabus, I calculated your final grade to be a B. If you have anything different for any of these grades or for the final calculation, please let me know, and I will be happy to discuss changing the final grade. But otherwise, it would not be fair to your classmates, who were graded according to the same criteria, to change your grade. Best of luck in the coming semester.

Tasha

Students with Persistent Complaints

If a student is persistent in their complaints and you are an assistant in a large lecture class, tell the professor about the situation as soon as you see that the problem is not going to be resolved easily. It is the professor's responsibility to support you or help you deal with this kind of situation. It is most helpful for the professor if you keep them apprised of the situation as it develops. Once you have talked with the professor and the student then says, "I am going to go talk to Professor Choi about this grade," you can say, "That is a good idea. Do you know how to get in touch with her?" This response will take much of the wind out of most students' sails or provide students a recourse if they truly feel the grade is unfair. If you are teaching your own class, alert the director of undergraduate studies to this situation.

If it becomes evident at any point in the semester that a student may complain persistently (and perhaps hostilely) about grades, keep a detailed record of your interactions with the student in case you need it at the end of the semester when it comes down to the final grade: photocopy papers with your comments, photocopy exams, take notes on meetings you've had with the student, and so on. You may never need to use this material, but you will be glad to have it if you do.

Letters of Recommendation

Because you often teach small classes of students and thereby come to know your students individually, students may regularly come to you asking for letters of recommendation.

Responding to the Request

When students ask you for letters of recommendation, be honest with them about how comfortable you feel writing such letters. Take every such request under serious consideration before agreeing or not agreeing to write a letter. You do not want to find yourself in the position of writing a letter for a student you cannot comfortably endorse.

GOOD STUDENT	If you know the student well, agree to write the letter with enthusiasm (students often are nervous about asking, and this will reassure them).
	Whether or not you know the student well, agree to write the letter but ask for additional materials (e.g., a résumé, a personal statement written for a graduate school application, a writing sample, a paper they wrote for you, etc.).
AVERAGE STUDENT	Decide whether or not you can write a helpful letter. If so, ask for additional materials if you need them. If not, ask the student whether there are other instructors who might be more familiar with their work and academic strengths.
POOR STUDENT	Ask the student whether there are other instructors they can ask—instructors who have seen their best work and perhaps know them better. If you need to, say that you do not think, given

what you have seen of the student's work, you
could write a helpful letter.

If you find yourself in the middle of trying to write a recommendation
and realize that you cannot honestly write a supportive letter, you need
to contact that student as soon as possible and advise that they seek out
another recommender.

Writing the Letter

If you agree to write a letter, ask for as many details as you can about
the position for which the student is applying and why they are applying—in other words, how they are going to use this letter. Ask for statements of purpose or résumés if you wish. The more specific and tailored
you can make the letter, the more helpful it will be. Show that you
know the student and describe unique, outstanding characteristics, if
you can. A few hints:

- Include specific details (e.g., an incident in class, a paper the student
  wrote).

- If you have minor reservations, include those also—they can make the
  letter more balanced and believable. However, remember that letters
  of recommendation tend to be "overinflated" across the board. Be
  extremely careful, therefore, in phrasing these reservations if you do
  not want the student's application to be adversely affected.

- Describe the student's "extracurricular self" if you know the student
  outside of class.

- Describe the student's work, communication skills, interaction with
  their peers and with you, goals and drive to achieve them, improvement, and so on.

- Compare the student's work with that of other students if it will
  highlight the student's strengths.

Include descriptive details whenever possible but still keep your letter pithy; potential employers and admissions committees want to be
able to find the important points of your letter quickly and easily. To
this end, front-load the paragraphs with the important points in case
the readers do not read the entire paragraph.

Ask when the student needs to have the letter mailed off and then meet this deadline. Feel free to ask students to provide you with stamped and addressed envelopes if they have not done so.

Keep electronic versions of all of your letters of recommendation on file. You often will find that you can tailor an old letter of recommendation to fit another student rather than starting from scratch.

See appendix G for sample letters of recommendation.

Further Reading

Davis, B. G. 1993. *Tools for Teaching.* San Francisco: Jossey-Bass.

Filene, P. 2005. *The Joy of Teaching: A Practical Guide for New College Instructors.* Chapel Hill: University of North Carolina Press.

Hodge, B. M., and J. Preston-Sabin, eds. 1997. *Accommodations—or Just Good Teaching? Strategies for Teaching College Students with Disabilities.* Westport, CT: Praeger.

Kottler, J. 1997. *Succeeding with Difficult Students.* Thousand Oaks, CA: Corwin Press.

Lambert, L. M., S. L. Tice, and P. H. Featherstone, eds. 1996. *University Teaching: A Guide for Graduate Students.* Syracuse, NY: Syracuse University Press.

Paludi, M. A., ed. 1996. *Sexual Harassment on College Campuses: Abusing the Ivory Power.* Albany: State University of New York Press.

Chapter 8
Grading

Grading is one of the most difficult and perhaps least enjoyable parts of teaching. Teaching assistants often spend too much time grading their students' work and worrying about it afterward. This chapter is designed to help you make the grading process more efficient, less stressful, and more fair to you and your students.

Grade Calculations

At the beginning of the term, you will want to determine the point values of all assignments and decide how those point totals will convert into a final grade. If you prefer to give letter grades rather than point grades on assignments, be sure to determine a point value for each letter grade (e.g., A+ = 100, A = 95, A− = 90, etc.) so that you have a basis for calculating final grades at the end of the term. At the beginning of the semester, let your students know how their final grade will be calculated; having a transparent grading system gives students a clear sense of where they stand in your course and helps you to be fair and accurate when assigning final grades.

If you plan to use a check/check plus/check minus system for more informal work, think ahead about how these scores will translate into a final grade for that part of the course. The same holds true if you are grading participation.

See appendix A for a detailed example of point values for assignments and how those points convert to a final grade.

Grade Books

When to Make a Grade Book

Wait about two weeks after classes begin before you create your permanent grade book; by then, most students have finished dropping and adding courses from their schedules. For the first two weeks, keep track of absences (and early grades, if applicable) on the attendance sheets provided by the department, in a temporary grade book, or by passing around an attendance sheet at the beginning of each class. You can usually acquire a grade book from your department or from a local bookstore.

How to Organize a Grade Book

Leave yourself plenty of space in the grade book in case you need to add revised grades, notes, or grade subtotals. It is easiest and clearest if you record absences and grades in different places. If the grade book has internal flaps, you can record grades on one flap and absences on another while using the same list of student names. Alphabetical order for students' names is a sure bet.

In recording absences, be sure to mark the date of absences in case students question their attendance or the participation part of the final grade. Also record late arrivals if a certain number of these is equivalent to an absence.

In recording graded material, set up columns for different kinds of assignments: papers, lab reports, problem sets, daily homework assignments, exams. Within each larger column, label individual columns for each assignment or exam. By grouping similar assignments in the grade book, you can more easily tally subtotals of the final grade and calculate their percentage of the final grade. In later sections of the grade book, you can reduplicate the class list and keep notes about students' progress, difficulties, successes, participation, and so on. These notes can be helpful at the end of the term in grading participation and in writing letters of recommendation.

Using Electronic Grade Books

Spreadsheet computer programs such as Excel or Claris make computing final grades a snap. The initial programming (e.g., creating the percentage values of each column) can take time, but at the end of the term, once all the grades are entered, the computer does all the math and does it accurately. If you use such a program, set up your columns exactly as you would in a traditional grade book.

Do not necessarily abandon the traditional grade book if you choose to use a computer program. Computers crash; programs (or you!) delete data. In addition, you can carry your grade book with you to record absences during class or assignment grades if you are grading somewhere other than next to your computer.

Preserving Your Records

Your grade book is a critical item, and its loss would be unpleasant for you and your students. To protect yourself and the grades, make photocopies of the grade book every couple of weeks so that you have backup records. If you're using a computer program, regularly back up and print out the records.

Once the term is over, keep the grade book at least two terms, if not longer. You will need these records if a student questions a grade. And these records can prove invaluable if a student later asks for a letter of recommendation.

Grading Exams

Exams can be some of the easiest material to grade because you (should) have a clear idea of your expectations and because all of your students are answering the same questions. When you sit down to grade a stack of exams, you should have a key to the exam that details the correct (or acceptable) answers and point values for each question. Ideally, you (or your professor) should write this key when you design the exam—this will help ensure that you have a good exam and that your questions have clear right answers (and no typos!).

Grading Logistics

Here are some hints that will save you time and answer many of your students' postexam questions.

- Every time you subtract points for an answer, write the number of points you are taking off next to the answer.

- Total the number of points taken off in each section or page and circle that total in the margin.

- Then, when you are calculating the final score, you can simply add the negative subtotals (which will be circled) for each section.

- Write, in brief, the correct answer next to the question when you take off points. You do not need to do this if you will review the exam in detail during class, if you will put an answer key on the course web site, or if the student made no attempt to answer the question.

- If you find yourself writing more on the student's exam than the student did, *stop!* Determine their final score, put the score at the top of the exam, and write next to it, "Come see me," or the equivalent. Then arrange a meeting with this student to find out what happened on the exam.

Grading Right/Wrong Questions

Questions that have right or wrong answers (multiple choice, fill in the blank, matching, etc.) are a cinch to grade as long as you know the point value for each question. If you are not going to go over these in class, you should write the correct answer next to each missed question, hand out a copy of the key, or post a copy of the key on the course web site.

Grading Short Answer Questions

Most short answer sections involve partial credit. You need to break down the answer and decide how much each part is worth. When you are grading, you can then subtract the given number of points for each part of the answer that is not included. Next to the subtraction, write (in a word or two) the idea that the student missed.

Grading Essay Questions on Exams

Grading essay questions on an exam can be a longer version of grading short answer questions. There are, however, some differences. First, decide what major points a student needs to include, how much each point is worth, and how much development of the idea you expect. Next, for each major point, decide how much credit you will give for partially developed answers and vague allusions to the idea in question. You may want to put a check mark next to each significant essay point as you grade.

If you let them, some students will write everything they know that might have anything to do with the correct answer to the question. To avoid this, when you hand out the exam, tell your students that you are aware of this exam-taking strategy. You may even confess to having used this technique yourself. Tell them that such answers are not suitable and that they should be sure to answer the exam question as it is posed to them. Tell students how short their answers can be; if you know that the correct answer only requires a couple of informed paragraphs, tell them so. Having said all this, you are not obligated to give full credit for run-on, buckshot essays.

Adjusting Class Scores

When you grade an exam, be attentive to questions that a great majority of students miss. If you come across one of these, look at the question again to be sure that it is fair. If it is not a fair question, consider dropping it from the exam or lowering its weight in the exam grade.

If all of the scores on an exam are low, the first thing to ask yourself is whether the problem is with the exam or with the students. If it is a problem with the exam, you may need to drop problematic sections from the total score or curve the overall score.

If the problem is with the students (you can usually tell that this is the case if a few students do well on the exam), do not feel you need to adjust the scores. Remember that low scores on tests before the final exam can provide motivation for students to work harder. What you do need to do is speak frankly with your students about their performance.

See "Handing Back Graded Material" in this chapter for more information on what to say when handing back exams with many low scores.

Grading Papers

Some students will complain that paper grades are subjective, and of course, they are to some extent right. But there are some objective standards of good writing. The clearer you can make these standards to yourself and to your students, the easier your grading will be. At the beginning of the term, give students a handout with summaries of your criteria for paper grades (you can attach this to the syllabus). Think about and write these criteria carefully because they are part of the course contract between you and your students.

An *A* Paper: A paper that is exceptional. It is interesting or unusual and demonstrates sophistication of thought. The main argument and supporting points are clear, complex, and well developed. The structure of the paper follows a clear, logical organization, and all sources are critically examined. It is free of grammatical and spelling errors.

A *B* Paper: A paper that is solid and fulfills the assignment. It has a clear argument but minor lapses in development. It touches on the complexity of the argument and shows careful reading of the sources. The structure follows a logical progression of ideas, but not all evidence is clearly related to the main ideas. It may contain a few grammatical usage problems but not enough to make reading difficult.

A *C* Paper: A paper that is adequate but less effective in responding to the assignment. It presents the central idea in general terms and demonstrates basic comprehension of the sources. It is difficult to find a logical structure to the argument, and the paper often relies on generalizations or unrelated examples. Sentences may be awkward or confusing enough to make reading difficult.

A *D* Paper: A paper that does not have a clear argument or does not respond to the assignment. The argument may be too vague or obvious to be developed, and there is little complexity in the ideas. The organization can be difficult to follow, and the paper offers insuf‹cient evidence.

An *F* Paper: A paper that does not respond to the assignment, has no central argument, and uses no sources. There is little apparent organization. There is no supporting evidence, or it is irrelevant.

Giving the Assignment

Tell your students as specifically as you can what you expect, both in terms of content and form, when you hand out or go over the paper assignment. It will not hurt to remind them of these criteria again closer to the due date.

Content

If you expect students to use outside sources, tell them; if you do not, tell them. If you expect to see a coherent argument/thesis, remind them (students sometimes believe that factual papers do not need an argument). If you want to encourage them to be creative, tell them. And whenever you can, provide examples. You can, for instance, describe to them the paper you might write if given this assignment and how you might organize it. In addition, be specific about page requirements (e.g., "approximately 5 pages does not mean 3 1/2 pages") or tell them the word length you have in mind.

Format

Give them strict guidelines about font and font size, about spacing, and about margin width—both at the sides and at the top and bottom. Tell them what personal information you need at the top: name, section number, date, assignment number, and so forth. And if you want the paper to have a title (other than, of course, "Assignment 2"), be sure to tell them.

Keeping Control of Grading Time

Grading papers can suck up as much time as you let it. You should not spend more than twenty to thirty minutes grading the standard under-graduate paper (four to seven pages). You are not doing yourself or the student any favors if you take more time than this. Keep a watch nearby and force yourself to check how long each paper is taking you. Make yourself speed up if you are taking more than half an hour per paper.

Taking less time will mean making fewer comments, but students cannot necessarily distinguish between the important and less impor-tant points in an extended barrage of comments. Concisely point out the next step the student should take in the improvement of their writ-ing, leaving later steps for your comments on the next assignment.

For example, if a paper is riddled with spelling and usage errors, the main argument is unclear, and the student misunderstood some of the sources, do not aim to comment on all of these problems. Begin by addressing the most fundamental problems—perhaps in this case the coherence of the argument. Then you can point out one major usage problem and tell the student you expect them to use the spell checker. In your comments on the next paper, you can then address the student's progress with these aspects of the paper and move on to the next step in improving the writing, perhaps the use of secondary material. It will help you to keep a summary of these comments in your grade book so that you can remember from paper to paper where students have been having difficulties. Alternately, you can ask students to attach previous papers and/or drafts (with your comments) when handing in their most recent assignment.

Choosing a Writing Implement

Unless you have a fetish for red, you may want to avoid red pens for grading. Red ink carries a lot of baggage for most students, and they will be more receptive to your comments if they are not red. Purple and green pens work nicely because the colors are dark enough to keep the writing legible; blue pens also can work if you are writing on typewrit-ten essays. Using a pencil is problematic because the lead smears over time and students can, if they are so inspired, change the grade or erase your comments. You do not want to run the risk of having a student alter a grade written in pencil and then approach you at the end of the term about a "miscalculation" in their grade.

Moving out of Problem Solving Mode

Problem solving is one of the biggest temptations and biggest traps in paper grading. When you read an essay that has, for example, serious organizational problems, your first reaction may be to figure out how to reorganize the essay so that it makes sense. This is not your job; it is the student's job. You can waste an enormous amount of time doing their work. Instead, you should tell them that the organization is weak and point out where and why. Ask questions; let them figure out the answers and how to fix the essay.

DON'T   "The organization of the argument is hard to follow. You talk first about X and then about Y. You then jump to Z. But X and Z are related, so why not talk about them together? It might work well to start with Y because it could tie in with your introduction. Z is clearly your strongest point, so perhaps you want to lead up to that. Then you could use the conclusion to tie back to the introduction. . . ."

Do   "The organization of the argument is hard to follow. You talk first about X and then about Y. You then jump to Z. Is there a logic to this ordering? Which ideas are related, and which are most important?"

DON'T   "In your argument for legalizing marijuana, you do not address the arguments against legalization. Many people would argue that legalizing marijuana will lead to greater use and to less concern about possible health risks. People may also stop making a distinction between cigarettes and pot. . . ."

Do   "In your argument for legalizing marijuana, you need to address the arguments on the other side of the issue. What points do people make in favor of keeping the present laws? How can you counter these? And what is the most effective way to organize these points and counterpoints when you revise this paper?"

Giving Feedback throughout the Paper

Begin by skimming through the paper to see the argument and get a sense of the organization (or lack thereof). Next, read the paper carefully with your pen in hand, commenting on ideas and marking specifically targeted areas of the writing. If you are going to grade several papers over the course of the term and you like to use abbreviated editing marks when you grade, provide students with a key at the beginning of the term so that they can understand what you have written on their papers.

A Guide to the Cryptic Marks on Your Papers	
ℯ	This word, space, or letter should be deleted.
¶	A new paragraph should begin here.
awk	This construction sounds awkward.
frag	This is a sentence fragment (i.e., it does not have a subject and a verb!).
sp	Spelling: this word is misspelled.
<u>a</u>	Capitalize this letter.
#	You need a space here.
quo status	These two words should be in the reverse order.
some one	This is one word.

Comments on Ideas

The margins are the ideal place to comment on smaller ideas within a paper because you will not have the time or space to mention them in the final comments. If a student makes a particularly good or specious argument, write a note there. If the student makes a confusing point, ask a question there.

Comments on Usage and Style

You cannot comment on everything, so try to be thematic. If the student is having problems with sentence fragments, mark those and do not try to mark all the sections that are consequently choppy. Focus on fixing one significant problem at a time.

If you are factoring grammar into the paper grade, seriously consider how much weight it should carry compared to the content of the work. Be especially careful about grading students harshly for usage "problems" that are debatable (e.g., split infinitives, ending a sentence with a preposition, singular generic *they*). And remember that a student's style and/or dialect may be very different from your own. At the same time, it is true that students' awkward written grammar can undermine the quality of their writing; use your comments to show them how they might construct sentences more effectively. Along these lines, consider substituting words like "effective" and "ineffective" for "right" and "wrong" in many circumstances.

Comments on Spelling and Typographical Errors

Do not waste time correcting spelling errors and typos. You can circle them as you see them, but you do not have to fix them. If these kinds of mistakes are particularly pervasive in a given essay, make a general comment on the need to proofread and, if appropriate, dock the grade for these mistakes. Students may not see the importance of ridding their papers of "little" mistakes unless they are penalized for them. You can explain to them that their readers may have trouble taking their argument seriously if it is presented sloppily.

Positive Comments

Do not write only negative comments or questions in the margins. If a sentence or paragraph is particularly well written, say so. If an argument is strong or well presented, say so. Students can learn as much from what they do successfully as from what they do unsuccessfully.

Feedback on the Whole Paper

The final comments are the time to address the "bigger picture" of the paper. Tackle the big things like the essay's argument, the organization, the major supporting arguments or facts, and the overall writing style. Leave the smaller points for the marginal notes. And remember that you do not have to solve the problems—your job is to point them out.

Scope

The key to writing good comments on students' work is striking the balance between too little and too much. Bear in mind how frustrated you have been over the years when you have put time into an assignment only to get it back with a grade on the last page. As importantly, remember that students can absorb only so much constructive criticism in one shot. Focus your comments on one or two major issues and perhaps one minor one (e.g., the style of the conclusion) and accept the fact that you cannot cover all the bases in your response to one assignment.

Form

For shorter assignments, writing your comments in the margins and on the last page often works well. For extended essays, teaching assistants generally opt to write a longer set of comments either on the last page or on a separate page stapled to the essay. For these longer sets of comments, it is helpful and kind (if a bit clichéd) to follow the "(Positive comment) but (Negative—yet constructive—comment)" formula.

EXAMPLE   "You set up the essay beautifully with the story in the beginning, and the conclusion nicely circles back to that story. But the organization of the paragraphs in between is not always clear. . . ."

Or you can use the first sentence to summarize the student's argument before you discuss its strengths and weaknesses. We recommend starting the comments by addressing the student directly and ending them by signing your name.

EXAMPLE   "Sarah,

You have chosen a provocative topic, and you clearly recognize the importance of including both sides of the issue. The next step is to think about how you want to organize these ideas. . . . I look forward to reading the next draft.

Jackie"

Legibility

In your comments, legibility is critical. It is incredibly frustrating for students if they cannot read your writing; if you do not write legibly, you might as well not write the comments at all.

If you choose to type your comments, be careful: some teaching assistants have found that their comments sound or become harsher when they type them, perhaps because they adopt the critical mind-set of their own academic work in front of the computer or, perhaps, simply because typewritten comments look and feel more impersonal. The advantage of typed comments is that you automatically have a record of your comments on all students' work.

Monitoring Student Progress

You may want to keep notes on your own comments so that you can cover different issues on each assignment. You can use pages in the back of your grade book for notes about each student, or you can keep them in a running computer file. You can also ask students to keep their papers and hand in all of the work they have done in your class with each new paper or at the end of the semester. Some teaching assistants warn students about their impending doom if they force the teaching assistant to comment on the same problem twice, but you should remember that the "same" problem can be difficult to define and a student's concerted effort to work on a problem may not be entirely successful.

Finding Your Grading Curve

You have to find the "zone" of grades that makes you feel comfortable and that is acceptable at your university. You want to be sure that you feel comfortable with the grades you give so that you can justify them to your students if you have to. That does not mean giving higher grades; it means understanding what you are conveying through each grade and what the student needs to do to get a higher grade.

Grading gets easier over time as you read more and more undergraduate papers. You acquire a better sense of the range of undergraduate writing and where a given paper falls in that range. And as you get more comfortable with grading, you will feel more confident about the grades that you assign.

Until you gain that confidence, there are strategies you can use to reassure yourself that each student receives the grade they have earned. It is usually easy to know how the papers in a class compare to each other, from the best to the worst. The hard part is knowing what grade that means each paper should get. Grading criteria can provide you with the guidelines and justifications for assigning particular grades. Obviously, if you feel comfortable assigning grades on papers as you go, this is an efficient and usually effectively accurate way to grade. If you are not yet at that point, you can try one of these strategies.

Strategy 1

Comment on the papers completely but do not put a grade on them. As you finish each paper, arrange it in the stack of graded papers from best to worst. When you finish all the papers, decide which papers (if any) deserve an A, which (if any) deserve an F, and where the rest fall in between. You will find that these decisions correspond to your criteria and that your grades are consistent.

Strategy 2

Comment on the papers completely and write the grade for each on a separate sheet of paper. You then have the flexibility to change a grade or the overall curve if you realize that you started out too low or too high. Once you are finished grading, go back and write each grade on the corresponding paper.

Allowing Revision

Students can learn a great deal from revising their papers, and it can provide your comments on a paper with a direct and immediate purpose. But grading all the revised versions can take a huge amount of your time. Here are a few suggestions.

- Set a limit on the number of papers a student can revise during the term.

- Set a time limit (e.g., two weeks) after you return a set of papers for accepting revised versions. This way, students must be organized and motivated to rewrite the paper; they cannot revise all their papers at the end of the term in a last-ditch effort to raise their grade.

- Warn students that their grades can go down as well as up on a revised paper.

- Establish guidelines for what constitutes "revision"; otherwise students may simply correct the punctuation and turn the paper back in.

- Ask students to turn in the original paper with the revision so that you can compare the two.

Grading Problem Sets

The first key to facilitating problem set grading is designing the assignment to be easy to grade. The goal of the entire assignment and of its parts should be clear enough that students know what is expected and you know what you are expecting.

Setting Guidelines for Students

Tell students explicitly how you want the problem sets formatted. You may want to provide examples on the board or on a handout. Some features to specify:

- whether the assignment should be typed or neatly written (in pen or in pencil);
- how big/small students can write and how much space they should leave;
- how they should identify the answer (circling it, etc.);
- how much explanation they should provide for steps within the problem (e.g., identify the theorem by name or spell it out);
- your policy on legibility (e.g., if you cannot read it, you will not grade it), decimal places expected, format, and level of detail.

Setting Point Values

Decide how many points each assignment is worth and how those points are broken down between the problems. Then determine how you will grade each problem by assigning the amount of credit students will receive for

- the right answer;
- the correct stages/methodology to move toward the answer;
- legibility.

Effort is clearly a subjective basis for grading, and if problem sets are not a major grade, you may choose not to use this as a criterion, or you may incorporate it as part of having the correct stages laid out in a problem. Explain to students how you assign point values at the beginning of the term or before a given assignment if the system changes for various assignments.

Logistics of Grading Problem Sets

Subtract points for each problem as you go. For obvious errors, circle the problem and write the point subtraction next to it. If you are taking off additional subjective points, write a short one-sentence or one-phrase comment to explain the error.

See "Grading Group Work" in this chapter for more information on grading problem sets completed by groups of students.

Grading Lab Reports

Setting Guidelines for Students

Lab reports will be easier for you to grade if your students understand your expectations for the content and format of the report.

See chapter 5, "Lab Reports," for more information on introducing lab reports.

Setting Point Values

Subdivide the points for each lab report as much as possible; this way, you can give credit for each part of the report the student completes correctly. Obviously, you will want to weight point values toward the interpretive sections of the lab report.

Logistics of Grading Lab Reports

Briefly read through all or at least several of the lab reports to determine how students did overall and where you may encounter problems. Once you begin grading, score each section of the lab report separately so that students see their strengths and weaknesses in the presentation of the results. Write the score for each section in the margin; you can then quickly calculate the overall grade at the end. In the following you will find advice for grading the different parts of lab reports.

Grading Descriptive Sections

For sections that address equipment, methods, and other standardized aspects of the lab, you can easily subtract points for missing information. Unless you will review the lab reports in class, briefly note what the students missed.

Grading Results

You need to decide how much it matters in the final lab report that the students achieve the results expected from the experiment. Remember, students with little understanding may get perfect results, while students with near-complete understanding may come up with the wrong results.

Grading Interpretive Sections

Interpretive sections (e.g., discussion of results, conclusions) require a combination of objective and subjective grading. Determine how much credit you will give for the correct answer(s). Then give yourself a range of points to award for the degree to which a student communicates their understanding of how the results relate to the broader goals of the experiment (this is where students can get credit for "effort"). If you subtract points for lack of understanding, do not feel compelled to explain the problem in depth in the margins; instead, write a question in the margin that directs the student toward the information they missed.

Grading Troublesome Sections

Occasionally the whole class will struggle in the write-up of one section of the experiment. When grading these sections, you may want to lower your expectations and grade more leniently. Then, if possible, review this section in class with all the students.

Grading Group Work

There are two general philosophies about grading group work: one grade for the entire group or different grades for each group member based on effort. Some instructors love group work. Other instructors feel that group work allows lazy students to ride on the coattails of their hard-working peers.

1. Each student in the group receives the same grade.

PROS   It is the easiest way to assign grades for group work.

It can encourage students to make the most of working as a group.

A combined grade reflects the "real world" consequences of a group effort: it is the final product, not the contributions of each group member, that counts.

CONS   Some students will put in more work than others, but they all will receive the same grade.

2. Each student's grade is based on their individual contribution to the group project.

PROS   Some students will put in more work than others, and their grades will be higher.

It can encourage students to work equally hard.

CONS   It can foster tension between group members because they are asked to judge each other's effort.

It is a more time-consuming way of assigning grades (see the directions that follow).

How to Assign Grades Based on Individual Effort

1. Determine an overall grade for the project.

2. Ask each student to turn in a list of the group members and their perception of the percentage of effort put into the project by each member. Remind students that the percentages should add up to 100 percent.

3. Average the percentages for each student.

4. Adjust each student's grade according to the percentage they contributed to the project. To do this, multiply the final grade (give it a

number value) by the number of students working on the project. Then for each student, multiply that number by the percentage of effort they contributed. Convert these numbers back to letter grades if necessary.

EXAMPLE   Overall project grade = B (3.0)

3.0 × 4 students = 12

All students about Student 1: 25 percent, 25 percent, 30 percent, 20 percent = 25 percent (make this calculation for each student)

Student 1: 25 percent × 12 = 3.0 (B)
Student 2: 25 percent × 12 = 3.0 (B)
Student 3: 35 percent × 12 = 4.2 (A or A+)
Student 4: 15 percent × 12 = 1.8 (C–)

Handing Back Graded Material

Each student's grades are between you and that student only. Never hand back graded material in a way that will compromise any student's confidentiality with regard to their grade (e.g., if you have arranged papers in order by grade, do not hand them back that way). For longer papers, put the grade on the last page with your comments or staple your typed comments to the back of the paper; you then can have students pass the papers to each other. For one-page assignments or exams with a grade on the top, be prepared to walk around the classroom and hand back the material to students individually or put the grade on the back of the assignment.

Handing Back Papers

Unless you intend to spend class time making general comments about papers, hand them back at the end of class. If you start by giving students their papers, they will read through your comments instead of paying attention, and students who got low grades may choose not to participate in class because they feel disheartened or because they wish to express a form of protest. Tell students at the beginning of class that you will be handing back papers at the end so that they do not leave early.

Prepare students for the grades. If you know the grades are generally low, tell them so and explain why and where many students had trouble. Explain the weight of this paper and what students can do to improve their grades. If you were disappointed with the papers, tell them so. If you were pleased, tell them so. Positive reinforcement can do wonders for class morale, and it can motivate students who realize their grades are falling below the class standard.

Positive and negative feedback to the entire class can motivate both stronger and weaker students, and it gives them some sense of where their grade fits into the range of grades in the class. Students also find it helpful to have some class or section statistics (e.g., mean, standard deviation, etc.) if they can be made available. Always remind students how they can reach you if they want to talk about their papers more than is possible during class.

Handing Back Exams

As with papers, unless you intend to spend class time reviewing the exams, hand them back at the end of class. Tell students the class average or range of grades so they know where they stand. If you are not running a review, briefly explain how you graded the exam and how students can reach you if they have questions.

Possible Climate Changes

Returning the first graded assignment can be the "end of the romance." Assigning grades can sometimes mark a shift in how your students perceive you and the class. Some of them may have seen you as a "friend" or "ally," and it can be jolting for them to be reminded that you give the grades and they get them. If there is a mood swing in the class with the first set of grades, it is almost always temporary—students rebound and remember that there are many assignments over the term and that the grading criteria are objective standards, not personal ones. Remember that the students are not disappointed in or angry at you; they are more often disappointed in their own performance. Keeping this in mind, do not feel that you need to apologize or to cater to their wishes for high grades or for a "teacher friend"; but do make it clear how they can improve their performance and how you can facilitate that.

In preparing your lesson plans, you may want to make sure that your classes that day and the next involve a high level of student participation so that students continue to feel invested in the success of the class.

> "In trying to explain to students how grades measure mastery rather than simply reward effort, I talk about the football team. I remind them that lots of players go to practice every single day and often practice even harder than the starting players, but they understand that this does not necessarily mean that they will get to start."

In-Class Review of Exams

There are times when you should devote part of a class period to reviewing exams because your feedback will apply to all the students. Reviewing an exam is a form of teaching: you will be reviewing or clarifying material that should be (but clearly isn't!) familiar to your students. Also, reviewing an exam in class can ease the work of grading: you only need to subtract points and not provide reasons on the exam itself.

When to Begin the Review

Unless you intend to spend the whole class period on exam review, you should always do an exam review toward the end of class. Once you hand back exams, students will be distracted and unable to focus on any other agenda. Decide how much time you will need to address the biggest problem areas of the exam and set aside that much time at the end of class.

Ending the Review

Another benefit of reviewing the exam near the end of class is that you have a clear-cut end to the discussion. If the class period ends before you have had the chance to address important questions brought up by your students, you can take more time to go over the exam during the next class meeting. If you have a few students with very specific questions, invite them to your office hours for a more tailored exam review.

How to Run the Review

After grading the exams, you will have a sense of the areas where students had trouble. You may want to begin the review by identifying the sections where most students did not have problems. Tell your class that you do not have time to review these sections but that, if they have questions, they should come talk to you after class or during office hours.

Take the section of the exam that gave students the most trouble and tell the students that many of them struggled with this section. You then can ask, "What do you think it is about this section that made it so hard for you?" This will get the discussion started.

Let the students help each other get the right answers. Moderate the discussion so that students listen to each other and do not get side-tracked.

Do not suggest to your students that they are dumb.

Don't "Other students have not had trouble with this exam in the past—there is no good reason why you all should have performed so poorly."

Do "I was surprised by the low scores. What do you think went wrong?"

"How did you study for this exam? What might change in your approach to studying next time?"

"Do you have thoughts about what we can do in class to make you feel more prepared for the next exam?"

Do more than just give out the answers.

Don't "Number one. The right answer is X. Number two . . ."

Do "Number one was definitely hard. What are some good examples you could have used to demonstrate the concept?"

"For number three, most of you knew that X was wrong, but you couldn't explain why. What thoughts do you have about it now?"

"For number five, many of you got the gist of the essay, but you were short on specifics. What important points belong in this essay?"

"For number seven, you had the facts for the essay but trouble organizing. Let's get those facts up on the board and figure out how to get them in an order that makes sense."

Make the review instructive, not humiliating.

Don't   Call on specific students for answers and force them to reveal their shortcomings to their classmates.

Do   Let students volunteer to answer questions with which they are comfortable or to contribute to an ongoing discussion of the correct answers.

Help students get the information they may be reluctant to request.

Don't   Make students ask about questions that they got wrong.

Do   Emphasize that certain questions were hard for everyone and initiate the discussion of these questions yourself. And always invite your students to ask about questions you have not addressed if time is still available.

Late Work

Most teaching assistants penalize students for turning work in late. If you have a strict due date, it is only fair to the students who turn in their work on time to take points off for late assignments. You should decide at the beginning of the semester how you will deal with late assignments and make your policy clear in your syllabus. For example, many teaching assistants subtract part of a grade for every day that an assignment is overdue. By outlining your policy in advance and sticking to it, you (and your students) will not need to worry about whether you are being unfair by penalizing students for late work. When you grade an assignment that has been handed in late, be clear in your feedback about how the grade was influenced by lateness as opposed to the quality of the work (e.g., "B → B– (late)").

Think carefully before adopting a "no late work accepted" policy. Imagine a scenario in which a good, conscientious student misses a deadline by an hour because the power went out and their final grade suddenly drops by a full letter because you must give them a zero for the assignment.

Missed Exams

The policy on missed exams may be dictated and announced by the professor of the course. If not, tell students in advance what will happen if they miss an exam. Given that students know the dates of the exams well in advance, it is not unreasonable to tell students that they should only miss an exam for illness or an emergency and that they should have proof of the reason for the absence. You can tell students that they will be allowed to make up an exam only if they bring you a note from a doctor or some proof of an emergency. If you are clear from the beginning of the semester that you have a strict policy about missed exams, you will be less likely to have students missing exams during the semester.

There are a few ways for a student to make up an exam.

- Write another exam that is sufficiently distinct from the one given in class and administer it to the student.

- Ask the student to write one or two short essays on topics that were covered by the exam.

- Consider the exam "missed" and double the weight of the following exam in the final grade.

What you do will depend on the nature and content of your course. What matters most is that you make your policy clear from the outset and that your policy does not unduly penalize students with a legitimate reason for missing the exam.

Calculating Final Grades

This often tedious process can be dramatically accelerated by using a computer program with mathematical capabilities. It can track scores throughout the semester, and it can quickly and accurately compute final grades once the last assignments are entered.

Calculating Class Participation

Regardless of how objective you make your grading over the course of the semester, calculating class participation is inherently subjective. The best approach is to grade students relative to each other on this dimension. However, consider all of the ways students can participate in the class and take these into account when calculating a participation grade. For example, a student may have said very little in class but may have been an active contributor to a class e-mail group. The grade should reflect the student's overall involvement in the course, not just their participation in group discussions. Calculating participation throughout the term can make the process easier and result in a more balanced assessment; two possible strategies are described in the following sections.

Grading Participation Weekly

One way to promote objectivity in grading participation is to make yourself grade each student's participation at the end of every week. This way, you can credit students for a particularly strong or weak performance that you may later forget. Then, at the end of the semester, you can average these weekly grades for an overall participation grade.

Having Students Grade Their Own Participation

In courses in which class participation is a critical part of the grade (e.g., foreign language classes), you may want to open a dialogue with students about their level of participation. On a regular basis (weekly or biweekly), you can ask students to submit a piece of paper on which they grade their own participation for that period and provide an explanation of the grade. You can return this paper during the next class meeting with your grade for them and an explanation of it. This way, students can be clear about your expectations and what they need to do to maintain or improve their participation grade.

Grading Final Exams and Papers

As you grade final work, particularly exams, bear in mind that for many courses, a significant number of students will not pick up the work once the course is over and they have received their grade. This does not mean that you should grade any less carefully, but you can limit your written comments. If you know that a student plans to pick up the work or has asked you to send it to their home, you can focus your efforts accordingly.

Returning Final Exams and Papers

Before the term ends, tell students how they can pick up or receive their final work. There are a few options.

- If appropriate, leave exams and papers with the support staff in your departmental office. Tell students that they can pick up their work during regular business hours.

- Schedule an extra set of office hours at the end of the grading period so that students can stop by to pick up their work.

- Tell students to turn in a stamped, self-addressed envelope with the exam or the final paper and you will mail the work to them.

We do not encourage you to leave a box of final work in the hall outside your office. This violates students' privacy and invites theft and destruction of property. Some universities even prohibit leaving student work in public areas like this. It is more difficult to schedule times and ways for students to pick up their work from you individually, but it is an important end to your contract with the students in the course.

Posting Final Grades

Now that final grades are often available to students on the Internet within days (or minutes) after you submit them, the need to post grades is becoming more obsolete. If you post grades outside your door, do so by student number (and make sure that the listing of numbers does not correspond to alphabetical order).

Further Reading

Davis, B. G. 1993. *Tools for Teaching*. San Francisco: Jossey-Bass.

Lowman, J. 1995. *Mastering the Techniques of Teaching*. 2d ed. San Francisco: Jossey-Bass.

McKeachie, W. J., and M. Svinicki. 2006. *McKeachie's Teaching Tips: Strategies, Research, and Theory for College and University Teachers*. 12th ed. Boston: Houghton Mifflin.

Stevens, D. D., and A. J. Levi. 2005. *Introduction to Rubrics: An Assessment Tool to Save Time, Convey Effective Feedback, and Promote Student Learning*. Sterling, VA: Stylus.

Walvoord, B. E., and V. J. Anderson. 1998. *Effective Grading: A Tool for Learning and Assessment*. San Francisco: Jossey-Bass.

Zak, F., and C. C. Watson, eds. 1998. *The Theory and Practice of Grading Writing: Problems and Possibilities*. Albany: State University of New York Press.

Chapter 9

Feedback from Students

Feedback from students, while it can be rewarding, also can be one of the more frightening parts of teaching. A good student is one who seeks out feedback, listens to it, and uses that knowledge to improve their performance. The same holds true for a good instructor. And while it can be stressful to ask students for feedback about the class, it is better for you to know their responses along the way rather than to wait until the end of term. Also remember that in the same way paper grades are about the student's work, not about the student, student feedback is about the course, not about your value as a person. This chapter will discuss ways to make student feedback as useful and constructive as possible.

General Informal Feedback from Students

At the beginning of the semester, tell your students that you would like them to keep you informed of their thoughts about the course throughout the term. Feedback always needs to be a two-way street. Encourage them to share their thoughts about the assignments, course discussions, lectures, readings, lab experiments, and class format. Sometimes it can feel like open-firing season when you create this space for feedback but remember you feel no more vulnerable than the students do when they turn in a paper to be graded.

Do not view this as a time to share your own anxieties about the course or to apologize for inexperience, workload, and so on. Simply tell students that you are interested in their feedback so that you can be sure they are learning effectively. This move (and your willingness to make it) will reinforce your authority in the classroom.

How Students Should Contact You

Let students know how they can give you feedback about all aspects of the course. You might encourage them to use e-mail, to drop a note in your box in the department, to stop by your office hours, or to bend your ear after class. If you would like students to be able to give you anonymous feedback, be sure there is a place where they can leave written notes for you throughout the semester.

Specific Informal Feedback from Students

It is not enough for you to tell students that you would like their feedback and to make the routes of communication available. You also need to solicit specific feedback throughout the semester.

Responses to Your Written Comments

Some teaching assistants have had success asking students to respond in writing to the teaching assistant's comments on a given essay or other assignment. If nothing else, this forces students to read the comments, and, at best, it helps them to process the critique and ask questions about comments that they do not understand. It can be a time-consuming process but often a worthwhile one.

If all your students have e-mail, you can require them to e-mail you within twenty-four or forty-eight hours with a paragraph response to your comments on their paper. In this way, you open up a dialogue about the paper and their writing. Be sure to give them some guidelines (e.g., they must ask at least one question or describe their plan for revision), or else you may get mostly praise for your insight (a.k.a. brownnosing in hopes that the next grade you give them will be better).

You also can ask students to write responses below yours on the papers themselves and turn them in at the next class meeting. You then will briefly respond to their comments and return the papers at the following meeting. You probably will want to keep notes in your files on their responses or ask them to turn in all previous work with each assignment so that you can target your comments more effectively on the next graded assignment.

Responses to a Discussion Section

It is not necessary (or feasible) to ask your students to respond to every discussion held in your class. However, there may be times when you have nagging concerns about a particular class discussion. If you feel uncomfortable with the way a discussion went, there is a good chance that several of your students also were aware that things did not go well. It is up to you to solicit feedback about what happened. At these times, "meta-teaching" strategies can be invaluable; see the following section for more details.

"Meta-teaching"

Meta-teaching means talking with your students about the teaching in your course as a way to teach them more. For example, if you felt that the last class meeting was marked by an unusually stilted discussion, have your students help you figure out why. While you may have to set aside your pride and admit that your class is no longer going as perfectly as planned, these are almost always fruitful discussions. In broaching the topic, you are reassuring your students that a bad class is not all their responsibility. It puts all of you on the "same team" in figuring out what might have stifled discussion and what can be done to improve the class dynamics.

EXAMPLE   "Last week we talked about the role of the voter in dictating international policy. Many of you seemed confused about how this discussion was relevant to the course. How can we relate it to the larger goals and topics of the course? What could we, or I, have done differently to facilitate a broader consideration of that topic?"

Some teaching assistants worry that meta-teaching will undermine their authority. In fact, the ability to use meta-teaching can demonstrate comfort with your authority in the classroom. Students respect teachers who are aware of and willing to address obvious problems.

DON'T   Use meta-teaching as a way of displacing responsibility for the success of the class (e.g. "I don't understand why you all won't talk in section. I've never had a group as uninterested as yours.").

Do   Use meta-teaching when it will be educational for the students to talk about what is happening in the classroom (e.g., "What does it mean that on Monday you all seemed uncomfortable talking about discrepancies in SAT scores along race and gender lines?").

Don't   Use meta-teaching to make the course about your insecurities or frustration with teaching; students should feel they are taking a well-planned course, not that they are part of an ongoing experiment (e.g., "I think I've figured out how to make all the groups more talkative. Last week I tried . . .").

Do   Use meta-teaching to address issues that seem to be particular to the material or to the students taking the class (e.g., recognize the complexity of a concept before trying to explain it, respond to unusually low exam grades).

Use meta-teaching to help students understand lesson plans and how they fit into the broader structure of the course (e.g., "In the last class, we talked about Kant's theories generally as a class. Today I'd like to begin by breaking you into smaller groups and having you dive into the text itself to look at the language Kant uses. I will give you some questions . . .").

Use meta-teaching freely.

You do not have to wait for a difficult discussion to use meta-teaching. The more that both you and your students participate in and reflect upon the teaching process as it unfolds, the more you will be able to involve students in learning. While it may feel a bit awkward for you and your students at first, feel free to recognize explicitly many of the dynamics of the class. Do not hesitate to introduce difficult material as difficult and challenge students to rise to the occasion. Do not hesitate to tell students when you are trying a new kind of class activity for them. Do not hesitate to recognize that a discussion may be sensitive or that students may be disappointed with their grades on a given assignment. As a general rule, you can legitimately and effectively give yourself the option of talking about and asking students about what they think is happening in the room as it is happening.

Formal Feedback from Students

Student conferences and written evaluations are ways to ensure that you will get student feedback. They can be very helpful for your teaching if you set them up effectively. If you will be using evaluations in the course, tell your students at the beginning of the semester; they can then prepare thoughtful feedback as the course progresses.

Midterm Conferences

Midterm can be a useful time to meet with each student individually to discuss their progress in the class and to get their feedback on the course. Bring a sign-up sheet to class with appointments scheduled fifteen or twenty minutes apart for each student to sign up for a convenient time.

At the conference, you need to be prepared with topics to discuss or to have asked students to prepare topics; you have asked the students to come see you, so you must try to make the conference productive. You can have notes ready on each student's work in the class and have a few questions to ask them about their experience in the class so far; these questions can be similar to those on a written midterm evaluation (see the following).

Written Midterm Feedback

Written midterm feedback is remarkably helpful in running a successful class or section. The feedback form can be fairly short (a half page, taking only ten minutes of class time); it still allows students to have some say in the content and direction of the course. Very few instructors ask their students what *they* want in a course, and students are generally appreciative and constructive when given this opportunity. These forms should be anonymous.

Writing the Questions

Ask questions that encourage students to be honest and take an active part in the shape of the course. Ask open-ended questions that require a response longer than "yes" or "no." You probably do not need more than four or five questions.

EXAMPLES   "I would like to see more/less time spent on _____."

"In the second half of the term, I would like to talk about _____."

"Written comments on my paper would be more helpful if _____"

See appendix H for sample midterm feedback forms.

Preparing the Students

Many students do not focus on the fact that you are going to read these feedback forms and that you have feelings too. Before you hand out forms, you may want to tell students that you will be reading them and that you take them seriously; you would appreciate all suggestions and constructive feedback they can provide. To encourage them to be honest, try to time the evaluation so that you are not holding papers or exams at the time. You do not want to "butter them up" so that they will only praise you and the course—you need to hear about what can be improved. But it is fair to remind students that you, a fellow human being, will be reading their comments so that they focus on being constructive instead of destructive if they have concerns to voice.

Talking About the Feedback

You must be sure to talk briefly about the feedback in the next class, after you have read the forms. The students need to hear you respond to their concerns and suggestions.

Examples "Many of you said that you found it useful when I put an outline of the lecture on the board, so I will try to do that consistently."

"A few students commented that we need to slow down when going over problems on the homework. I will try to ask if we're all on the same page as we go, but please let me know if I'm going too fast."

"A couple of students wrote that they wanted to read more poetry. I'm afraid that I cannot work extra reading into the syllabus, but I would be happy to give any of you recommendations on outside reading if you're interested."

Written Final Evaluations

Standardized Evaluations

At almost all universities, you will be asked to have students fill out a standardized evaluation form at the end of the term. Many of these ask students to rate aspects of the course and the instructor on a numerical scale; while there are bureaucratic and pedagogical reasons for these evaluations, numerical ratings will not necessarily help you improve your teaching or the course. Tell students that you are looking for feedback specific to your course and you would appreciate their taking the time to write comments on the back of the evaluation.

Supplemental Evaluations

If it is at all feasible, you should write your own evaluation form to enhance the standardized process. Such an evaluation will be particularly useful if you will be teaching the same or a similar course again. Write questions similar to those on the midterm evaluation.

Reading Your Evaluations

Prepare yourself for the fact that reading evaluations can be anywhere from exhilarating to devastating—or both. There almost always will be some negative evaluations in the stack (often from students not doing well in the course), and any number of positive evaluations does little to ease the immediate sting of a student's criticisms. Students may even bypass the course content and go straight for your feelings; students have been known to tell instructors to get new haircuts, buy new clothes, and/or "get a life." These students are usually venting academic frustration in destructive ways; do not let their anger make you question your teaching abilities.

However, you should take consistent negative feedback on a particular aspect of the course very seriously. While your feelings may be hurt, you need to use the students' comments as a way to improve your teaching and/or the course.

Here are a few ways to keep the negative evaluations in perspective.

- Reread the positive ones and remember that not every student is going to like your course or teaching style.

- Tell a friend or family member about the bad ones so that they can reassure you that these evaluations happen to everyone and you are still a wonderful person, even if parts of your teaching need to be improved.

- Remember that one course does not make or break your teaching career. Learning to teach effectively is an ongoing process, and there is no reason to expect yourself to be perfect every step of the way.

- Try to see the negative but constructive comments in the perspective of the comments that you write on students' work. You are trying to help them improve and do not intend the comments to be hurtful or personal.

- Remember that even the best teachers have had students criticize their teaching, their grading, their clothes, and even their hairstyles!

Before reading the evaluations, set up your day appropriately.

DON'T   Read them right before teaching or even going to a class of your own.

DO   Read them in the comfort of your home or with a friend, if you want moral support.

Read them with a cup of your favorite coffee, a bag of chips, or a box of cookies, depending on your comfort food of choice.

Read them.

Read your evaluations because you will learn a lot and you will improve the course. But be nice to yourself too.

"When I got back my evaluations after my first semester of teaching, I ripped open the envelope and started reading. I read through twenty-one fine, good, and even wonderful evaluations, and then I got to the last one: there were low scores in every category, and on the back, the student had written, "I think Joanna is annoying. And it would help if she understood the material." I was devastated. And I couldn't imagine how I was going to walk into the classroom and start teaching . . . in five minutes!"

Further Reading

Angelo, T. A., and K. P. Cross. 1993. *Classroom Assessment Techniques: A Handbook for College Teachers.* 2d ed. San Francisco: Jossey-Bass.

Brookfield, S. D. 1990. *The Skillful Teacher: On Technique, Trust, and Responsiveness in the Classroom.* San Francisco: Jossey-Bass.

Davis, B. G. 1993. *Tools for Teaching.* San Francisco: Jossey-Bass.

Lowman, J. 1995. *Mastering the Techniques of Teaching*. 2d ed. San Francisco: Jossey-Bass.

McKeachie, W. J., and M. Svinicki. 2006. *McKeachie's Teaching Tips: Strategies, Research, and Theory for College and University Teachers*. 12th ed. Boston: Houghton Mifflin.

Chapter 10
The Balance of School and Teaching

One of the hardest parts of graduate school is balancing your duties to your students and your duties to yourself and your own education. Most graduate students feel that they could work full-time on any one of their multiple obligations and still not get as much accomplished as they would like. This chapter suggests ways to integrate teaching into your demanding graduate program.

Front-Loading Effort

The better prepared you are for the course at the beginning of the semester, the less work you will have during the semester. If you have control over the syllabus, write a detailed one that guides you from week to week. In addition, take advantage of the lull in your own course work at the beginning of the semester to run lab experiments, to make copies of long handouts, or to complete other foreseeable time-consuming tasks.

Assigning Responsibility

Your job as a teaching assistant is to guide the learning of your students, not to do their work for them. While you should recognize that college course work can be demanding for many students, you should not feel obligated to tailor an individual course of study for each of your students. Ironically, the students who demand the most of your time are often the students who put the least effort into the course. Resolve that you will not do more work for a student than the student is doing for your course.

Here are a few ways to make sure that you do not take too much responsibility and that your students take enough.

• Write a clear and complete syllabus.

Use it as a way to tell students what you will do for them and what they are expected to do for the course. Establish clear guidelines for what will happen when students fail to do their work and stick to them.

DON'T   "Late work will be penalized."

Do   "Paper grades will be lowered by five points for every day late."

DON'T   Assume that every student will feel they have to come to every exam.

Do   "Contact me in advance if you will not be able to attend an exam and need to arrange a makeup. If you do not attend an exam and do not contact me in advance, you will need to provide proof of an emergency in order to take a makeup."
         See chapter 2, "Establishing Contact" and "Syllabus: Setting the Agenda," for more information on developing your syllabus.

- If a student is struggling in your course, be clear with the student about what *they* must do to get back on track.

DON'T   If a student has missed three weeks of class, offer to meet with them individually to summarize the material.

Do   If a student has missed three weeks of class, explain where the information can be found (the course pack, a friend's notes, etc.) and offer to answer specific questions once they have read over the material.

DON'T   Devise a complex plan for how a student can make up missed work.

Do   Ask the student how they feel they should make up the missed work. They will invariably devise a more demanding and cruel plan than anything you would ever have come up with!

Student: I was in Florida over spring break, and I got so badly sunburned that I haven't been able to come to class for three weeks. What did I miss, and how can I make it up?

TA: Sorry about the burn. In the last three weeks, we have covered chapters five through ten in the text, the middle third of the course pack, and we have taken two in-class quizzes.

> *Student:* Wow, I missed a lot. What can I do to make it up?
>
> *TA:* You're right: that is a lot. What do you think would be a good way for you to get completely caught up with the material?
>
> *Student:* I guess that I could copy a friend's notes, write brief summaries of all the chapters and articles, and write a short paper that covered the material on the quizzes. Does that sound okay?
>
> *TA:* That sounds fine. Show me the chapter and article summaries and give me the paper to grade. I'll give you two weeks from today to hand them in.

- Schedule your office hours so that they have a distinct ending.

You are not obligated to meet with students past the time of your scheduled office hours if you do not want to. Do not hesitate to point out to the student kindly that office hours are ending; do not feel that you need to justify doing so. Invite the student to come to your next scheduled office hours should they wish to.

Scheduling Teaching-Related Activities

Teaching Classes

You may not have a choice about when you teach your classes. But you may have the option of meeting with all of your classes on one day or of spreading the classes throughout the week. Whatever you choose to do, try to schedule your sections so that they all occur after the same lecture. This way, you need to create only one lesson plan per week. Many teaching assistants prefer to teach all of their classes on the same day, and there are both pros and cons for doing so.

PROS   You will save time by only needing to assemble your teaching materials once each week.

You can get into a "teaching mode" and stay there as you move from one class to the next.

You can make small changes and correct mistakes you see in the class plan.

You can minimize "downtime," as many teaching assistants find that they are not able to do much of their own work right before or right after they teach.

Cons   Teaching can be exhausting, so you may run out of energy before you get to your last class.

If you find that you are missing necessary materials, or that you need to develop a different class plan altogether, you will not have time to make major adjustments before you get to your next class.

A bad first class may affect how you feel about teaching later ones.

Preparing for Class

Be sure to set aside time each week just for teaching preparation. You probably will want to do this at least a couple of days before the class so that you will have time to get any needed materials or to photocopy any handouts. Schedule this time in your planner; it is more efficient and less stressful than trying to cram your preparation in around the edges of your other work. If you want your students to prepare before they come to your class, be sure to get one or two weeks ahead in your class planning so that you can tell them what will be expected week to week.

Making Your Schedule

When you choose to block out preparation and grading time in your schedule will depend on how you function both as a teacher and as a student. A few suggestions:

- Figure out when you do your most productive academic work (be it early in the morning or after midnight) and leave those times available.

- Determine whether you can use postteaching downtime as a time for grading or for class preparation. Devoting certain days to teaching and others to your work can be an effective division of time.

- Schedule your blocks of time with natural breaks to end them (e.g., meals, sleep, scheduled activities like exercise). This will make it easier for you to stick to your schedule and to keep your activities distinct.

Monday	Tuesday	Wednesday	Thursday	Friday
8–11 Grad. courses	8–11 Teaching prep.	8–10 Grad. courses	9–11 OFFICE HOURS	9–12 Grading time
11–5 Grad. course work	11–1 Free time!	10–12 SECTION 1	11–1 Free time!	12–1 Free time!
	1–5 Grad. course work	12–1 Lunch	1–5 Grad. courses and course work	1–5 Misc. work time
		1–3 SECTION 2 3–5 class prep./ notes on teaching		

Coordinating Teaching and Personal Schedules

In graduate school, you must learn to be a student *and* a teacher and still feel like you have time to be human.

Sharing the Burden

You owe it to your students to be prepared for every class, to be familiar with all of the material, and to take them and their work seriously. You also owe it to yourself to take advantage of opportunities to do less, not more, work. Here are a few suggestions.

- Ask your students to prepare review questions before an exam and help them work through the answers as opposed to developing a review sheet for them.

- Ask your students to take responsibility for giving presentations to their classmates at the end of the semester.

- Ask several students to come to class prepared with a discussion question about a text so that you do not have to devise all of the questions.

- Invite a guest speaker.

Employing such strategies will significantly lighten your teaching load because you will be asking students to take partial responsibility for leading the class. And it may even improve your teaching as students become more active learners.

Scheduling Due Dates

If you have control over when your students will hand in papers, exams, or problem sets, try to schedule these at times when you will not be working on significant papers, exams, or problem sets of your own. Then schedule uninterrupted grading times and uninterrupted work times for yourself throughout the week; protect those times jealously! Do not schedule meetings with students or professors during your work times; do not let yourself grade during your work times. And if you finish grading early in a scheduled block of grading time, give yourself the rest of the scheduled block as "free time."

"When I first started as a teaching assistant, I was all too willing to accommodate the schedules of my students, even if it was inconvenient for me. I had one student who could never make my regularly scheduled office hours but who often wanted to meet. I would usually agree to meet at a time he suggested, even if I knew that it meant walking from one side of campus to the other and then back again after our meeting. I am now more careful about when I agree to meet with students. If you take a few extra minutes, you can often find a time that is convenient for both of you."

Self-Preservation

You would not be a graduate student if you did not hold yourself to high standards in your academic life. Many graduate students feel that they should be as good at teaching as they are at learning. It is easy to forget that you have spent at least sixteen years of full-time work honing your skills as a student. It is also easy to forget that if you stay in academia, you will spend your career perfecting your skills as a teacher; even the most talented and experienced teachers learn and develop new skills all the time.

Enjoy Your Successes

Be sure to recognize things that are going well in your classes and take credit for them. Do not assume that you are responsible only for the things that go poorly.

Expect and Accept Your Failures

Things will not always go well. You will have difficulty dealing with some students. Some of your discussions will go better than others. Students will ask you questions for which you are not prepared. You will have days when not one of your students will have something helpful to contribute to the class. You will have class plans blow up in your face.

Some of the things that go wrong in your class will be because of the students; some will be because of you; and some will result from a misalignment of the stars. All good teachers have bad days, and there is such a thing as an awkward group of students who will not come together to learn no matter what you do. Expect that you will make mistakes and take time to figure out what went wrong. Make notes on your class plan about what happened so that if you ever use it again, you will be able to make changes. The sooner you accept that things will not always go well, the sooner you can use your mishaps to guide you to better teaching in the future.

See chapter 9, "Responses to a Discussion Section," for more information on how to walk back into the classroom after a bad day.

Think of Teaching as a Process

Teaching is like driving. Even though you likely got your driver's license when you were sixteen, you are a better driver now (we hope!) than you were when you first were let out on the road. Graduate students teach because they are more familiar with the material than the undergraduates. Other than that, there is no reason why a graduate student who has never taught before should be a perfectly skilled teacher. You will continue to develop and learn as a teacher with every semester, but to begin, you will just have to take the wheel and start driving.

Appendixes

Sample Course Syllabus

Psychology 101
INTRODUCTORY PSYCHOLOGY

Teaching Assistant: Frances Francini
Office: Room 2301 Big Hall
Office Hours: M & Th 10–11 (If you cannot make these hours,
please feel free to make an appointment.)
Psychology Dept. Phone: 555-6333 (You can leave a message.)
E-mail Address: fran@theuniv.edu (checked daily)

COURSE DESCRIPTION: The goal of this class is to introduce you
to psychology as a field and to familiarize you with the practice,
principles, research methods, and controversies of the divisions
within psychology: clinical, social, cognitive, organizational, devel-
opmental, and biological.

GRADING: Your final grade will be calculated based on a semester
total of 600 points:

Paper one = 100 points
Papers two and three @ 50 points each = 100 points
Multiple-choice practice questions, worth 5 points each = 60 points
Three tests, worth 100 points each = 300 points
Participation in class discussion = 40 points

A = 600–560	C+ = 479–460	D– = 379–360
A– = 559–540	C = 459–440	F = 359 and below
B+ = 539–520	C– = 439–420	
B = 519–500	D+ = 419–400	
B– = 499–480	D = 399–380	

ATTENDANCE AND PARTICIPATION: You will be allowed two
absences during the semester. Your section grade will go down by
2% for each additional absence. Exceptions may be made for significant (and documented) emergencies and illnesses—a broken alarm
clock does not qualify as a significant emergency (sorry). Your participation grade will be based on your contributions to class discussions and/or your demonstration of participation in the course
through visits to office hours, contributions to class e-mail discussions, etc.

GROUP PRESENTATIONS: The group presentations will be due on November 23. Each group presentation will last for about ten minutes. An informational sheet on the group presentation will be handed out in class on November 9.

PAPER: Your papers should be 4–5 pages (double-spaced) in length. More detailed descriptions of the papers will be handed out on Sept. 21. Papers will be graded down by one half-grade for every day that they are late.

PLAGIARISM: Plagiarism is the act of presenting other people's work or ideas as your own. If you are suspected of plagiarism, your work will likely be forwarded to the college's academic judiciary. Plagiarism can result in suspension or expulsion from the university. If you have any questions about how to reference material or about what constitutes plagiarism, please come see me.

SCHEDULE

Sept. 13   The Development of Psychology as a Field
                   Reading: Textbook, Chapter 1
       20   Social Psychology
                   Reading: Textbook, Chapters 2 & 3
                   Paper assignment #1 will be handed out.
       27   Biological Psychology
                   Reading: Textbook, Chapter 5
                   * Bring two copies of paper draft to section.

(And so on)

Appendix B
Lesson Plan for a Discussion Class

GOAL: Ensure that students understand findings of recent research on the neurochemical basis of aggressive behavior and explore the social and ethical implications of this kind of psychological research

LESSON: Review research readings, ask students to design studies that highlight the limits that ethical practice places upon scientific research, and explore broader ethical questions in this area

1. Class business:
   - Assign articles for next week's information exchange
   - Have each student write down a question about yesterday's lecture on an index card; collect these and ask a few people to volunteer questions (we'll talk about the others next week)

                                                     (10–15 minutes)

2. Review of recent research on the impact of noradrenaline and serotonin on aggressive behavior (let's do this together to make sure we're all on the same page):
   - Two students at board as the classmates share ideas: one student writing list of what we know about the relationship; one writing list of what we still do not know

                                                         (10 minutes)

3. Group activity: In groups of three, come up with a study that would elaborate on our current understanding of the relationship between noradrenaline, serotonin, and aggressive behavior but would be unethical.

                                                            (8 minutes)

4. Discussion based on activity: Have groups share their study and their ethical concern about it.
   - Do others agree that such a study would be unethical?

                                                        (20 minutes?)

5. More general discussion (if time):
   • Should different ethical standards be applied to human and animal research?
   • Some would argue it is not "good science" to use results from animal studies to make assertions about human behavior. Do you agree? Why or why not?
   • If a drug did exist that drastically reduced aggressive behavior in humans, should it be made available for use? If so, on whom? Under what conditions, if any, could a person be required to take the drug?

6. Wrapping up:
   • Relate student points to the next set of readings about ethical science
   • Remind students of expectations for information exchange

Appendix C
Lesson Plan for a Lecture Class

GOAL: Help students understand Kohlberg's stages of moral development and how they relate to real-world situations

LESSON: Begin with a lecture to briefly review the textbook descriptions of Kohlberg's stages; have students participate in moral reasoning activity; use board to match the students' examples of moral reasoning to the appropriate Kohlbergian stage.

- Class business:
  - alert students to change in date of makeup exam
  - hand back stray papers from last week

1. Review textbook definitions for each of Kohlberg's stages: (10 minutes)
   - Preconventional morality
   - Conventional morality
   - Postconventional morality

2. Put students into pairs, give handout, have each pair of students (10 minutes)
   - Decide which of the worthy students described in their handout should receive a coveted scholarship.
   - *Write out their reasons* for why they chose the student they did.

3. Have each pair share their decision and the reasoning behind their decision. Write the reasons on the board. (15 minutes)

4. Return to definitions of each of Kohlberg's stages and have students help to match the varieties of reasoning on board to the appropriate Kohlberg stage. (15 minutes)

5. Conclusion: Remind students that it is the nature of the moral reasoning, not the actual decision, that matters in Kohlberg's theory. Prepare students for next week's look at Carol Gilligan's response to Kohlberg's theory. (5 minutes)

Appendix D
Annotated Text with Questions

Text:

neg. connotations — statement (not opinion)

Sexual harassment involves an (abuse) of power. Teachers always have more institutional power than students; students sometimes have more physical or cultural power than teachers. Sexual harassment between teachers and students can go both ways. Instructors may be sexually harassed by students, but it usually happens the other way around. ── a warning to the audience

Sexual Harassment by Teaching Assistants

the transition to more specifics   necessity

You are in the position of authority with regard to your students; you (must,) therefore, be especially careful not to abuse your power. Many teaching assistants are close enough in age to their students that they may flirt with the idea of having a romantic encounter with one of them. These thoughts may be fueled by the fact that students often have crushes on their teaching assistants. (Under no circumstances) should you pursue a romantic and/or sexual relationship with a current student. In addition, you should (never) do (anything) that might be construed by a reasonable person as a sexual advance.

Questions:

- What tone is established with the first sentence? Which words jump out at you?
- How do the authors shift tone (and audience) in the second paragraph by starting with the word *you*? Why do you think they do that?
- Circle the language in the second paragraph that stresses necessity. How does this make you feel as the reader?
- How do the authors establish their authority?
- Why have the authors chosen to present the perspectives of both teachers and students?

- The organization reflects a movement from general observations to specific advice. How would the text read differently if it started with the second paragraph?

Appendix E
Guidelines for a Paper Workshop

Workshopping in Groups[1]

The goal of a peer workshop is to help the writer of an essay see what aspects of the essay still need work and to suggest possible approaches to the essay's revision. It is a time for the writer to work directly with the audience to make the essay as effective as possible.

Readers: You are the audience of this essay, and it is your task to help the author achieve his or her desired reaction to the essay. The workshop is *not* a time for you to read your response verbatim to the author; he or she can read the response later. The workshop is a time to *talk* with the author about your reaction to the essay, about the author's concerns, about areas you think need more development, about ideas you did not understand, etc.

As the audience, you should tell the author how the text "reads." Your response to an essay cannot be "wrong" because it is your opinion. It is helpful to the author to know how readers are responding, and he or she can decide whether or not to revise the essay to avoid or heighten this reaction.

Focus on the essay's argument and main ideas. Talking about the argument of an essay is more valuable than talking about the details of the prose because after revision of the argument, the prose of the text may be drastically altered. Ask yourself, what are the two or three things I can say which will help this essay the most? Matters such as purpose, tone, perspective, large-scale organization, and logic should be first on the agenda. Do not ask the writer to accept or reject any suggestion on the spot. You are simply suggesting possible alternatives, which the writer can mull over.

Authors: Most of us have trouble responding well to criticism of our own writing. Writing can be a personal act, and an essay can become an object of affection and of almost parental pride. It can be difficult to separate criticism of the essay from criticism of our ideas and from criticism of ourselves.

Approach the workshop with a positive mind-set; remember that the session is for your benefit and will help you improve the essay before it is graded. You can set the tone for the workshop; if you seek out constructive advice, you will usually elicit it.

Try to avoid becoming overly defensive; if you argue away all your readers' reactions and suggestions, you defeat the purpose of a workshop. If you find yourself feeling defensive, take control of the conversation and start asking questions about the aspect of the essay—questions you know will help you in revision. Create a situation in which you feel your readers are working *with* you on the paper, not against you.

Do not feel, however, that you must accept every suggestion from your readers unquestioningly. Sometimes your readers' responses will be contradictory or confusing. Ask them to explain or elaborate. You are the one with an intended purpose for the essay, and only you can accomplish it. Your readers can help you see where you have gone astray, especially if you explain your goals to them.

Group Dynamics: You will be working in groups of three. Do not work from your written responses for the in-class workshop; instead, use your copy of the draft (which should already have your comments on it) as the basis for discussion. It often works well if the writer controls the discussion, at least in the beginning, but if the writer does not feel comfortable with this role, one of the readers should get the ball rolling. Your group should spend about twenty minutes on each paper, which should be enough time for you to discuss each paper thoroughly.

If you are looking for some structure, here are a few basic questions you can use to guide your discussion.

1. What did the readers see as the essay's argument? What was the author's intended argument? If these are different, what has gone awry?
2. Is the argument focused enough? Is it developed enough? In other words, does the author need to push his or her ideas one more step?
3. Does the author fully support and develop the argument? Do all the main ideas support the argument? Do any need more detail?
4. Is the organization of the essay clear? Are there transitions between ideas/paragraphs? Are the author's ideas easy to follow?
5. Are there any paragraphs which do not have a clear function within the essay as a whole?

6. Are there any generalizations in the essay you thought were unsupported or weak?
7. Was the author's tone in the essay effective? Was his or her diction (word choice, style, etc.) appropriate to the subject?
8. Did the introduction get your attention? How is the transition from the introduction into the argument? Does the conclusion do more than regurgitate what already has been said?
9. Does the author have any remaining questions?

[1]Adapted in part from Jack Rawlins, *The Writer's Way,* 2d ed. (Boston: Houghton Mifflin, 1992).

Appendix F

Guidelines for Writing a Peer Response

Peer Reviews

1. Read through your classmate's paper once without stopping. It is important to get the big picture of the essay before you focus on the individual parts.

2. Reread the essay with a pencil/pen in hand and make notes in the margins or between the lines with your thoughts or questions about the author's ideas, organization, or anything else you notice. Note: this stage of the writing process is not the time to be proofreading, because the author probably will make major changes to the entire paper, not to mention the individual words and sentences. Focus instead on the paper's organization, paragraph structure, supporting details, transitions, etc. You will be using this marked-up draft in the workshop discussion, and you will be giving it to the author.

3. Respond to the following set of questions. You can either frame the response as a letter to the author, making sure that you cover all this ground, or you can write a coherent paragraph or more about each aspect of the paper. Your response should be 1–1 1/2 pages long, single-spaced. Make your comments as constructive and specific as you can so that the author can use them to improve the paper. Provide positive feedback along with constructive suggestions. Print out two copies (one for the author and one for the instructor) and bring them to the workshop; put your name on top and then the title of the paper and the author.

A. Argument: Restate the paper's argument and then evaluate its effectiveness. For example, you can discuss whether you found the argument interesting and/or provocative or whether it does not push far enough beyond the fairly obvious. If you had trouble identifying the argument—perhaps because there are multiple arguments or the paper remains in generalities—help the author see where you had problems.

B. What's Working? Help the author see what is working really well in the paper, so that he/she is sure not to lose that in revision.

C. What's Not Working Yet? Help the author see where you struggled when reading the paper, perhaps because a point isn't clear or evidence is not clearly related to the overall argument or the organization is hard to follow, etc.

In these general categories, here are a few things you should be sure to cover:

- **Evidence:** Which claims need more evidence, more detail, or more support in order to be convincing? Where is evidence not clearly linked to specific claims? Where are there generalizations without specific evidence?
- **Detail:** Where would more detail usefully illustrate an author's point?
- **Organization:** Can you explain the organization of the paper in a way that makes sense? If not, where did you get lost, and how might this be rectified? Identify any parts of the paper that you thought were repetitive or unnecessary.
- **Introduction:** Does the introduction make you want to keep reading? If so, could you also determine the focus as well as perhaps the argument of the paper? Can you suggest ways to make the introduction clearer and/or more interesting?
- **Conclusion:** In what way does the conclusion do more than regurgitate the argument of the paper? Could it do more, or should it do less?

Sample Letters of Recommendation

A. For an excellent student whom you know well

January 17, 2007

It is a true pleasure for me to write this letter of recommendation for Sandra Garcia, who was my student in Sociology 115, "Introduction to Sociology," in the winter term of 2006. Sandra is, without question, one of the four or five most outstanding students I have taught at Big State University in six semesters of teaching.

Sandra is a careful and creative thinker with an eye for details and a devotion to logic, which serves her well both in the sciences and outside them. She has the terrific ability to draw on her own experience and observations to develop thoughtful opinions on a variety of issues. Sandra already knew she wanted to major in biology when she took my course, but this did not diminish her intellectual curiosity about the topics we covered in introductory sociology. Her regular contributions to full-class discussions provided insight both for her peers and for me as an instructor.

Sandra was also invaluable in small-group interaction with her peers. Without my asking, she took on the responsibility of helping her classmates consolidate vast amounts of information into coherent sets of ideas, and she quickly became a study group leader. In addition, Sandra was very generous with her time and energies. I remember her meeting individually with a student from Thailand several times before the final exam to help him master all the material in a foreign tongue.

Sandra breaks the "scientist" stereotype with her writing: she was the best writer in the two sections I taught that semester. And what was perhaps even more impressive was that she took the task of improving her writing as or more seriously than any other student in the class. One of her essays was later published in the annual magazine of the best undergraduate essays written in sociology.

Sandra is not only an excellent student, but she is also personally delightful. She is as comfortable with herself as she is engaging, pleasant, and humorous. As I got to know Sandra over the semester, I became only more impressed by the wide range of her abilities—and by her modesty about them. She is an accomplished musician and scientist, both of which she does with a passion rare in undergraduates.

I wholeheartedly recommend Sandra as a prospective medical school student. In fact, I can think of few students whom I would recommend as highly. She will add a great deal to any incoming medical school class. I can also envision Sandra as a highly competent and caring doctor someday, which I say as a high compliment indeed. Please contact me if there is anything else I can do on her behalf.

Sincerely,

Peter Severs, M.A.

Peter Severs, M.A.
Graduate Student Instructor

B. For a good student whom you do not know well

5 January 2007

I am pleased to recommend Natasha Kincaid for admission to the Teacher Education Program. Natasha was my student in Biology 210 (Cell Biology), and she proved to be a model student. She is extremely conscientious about her work and about attending class and lab. Because of her hard work, she consistently scored in the top ten percent on all the exams and problem sets. Her work demonstrates an attention to detail and an ability to integrate material to create larger frameworks for discussion.

Natasha made intelligent and insightful contributions during full-class discussion, but it was in lab that her enthusiasm and teaching abilities shone. After the first week, she became the leader of her lab group, and I would often see her patiently explaining a procedure or a concept to her lab mates (and often those in the neighboring lab group as well!). She took the initiative to organize and lead class reviews before the exams, and other students told me afterwards how helpful these sessions were.

I believe that Natasha's strong academic abilities and her clear dedication to teaching make her a very strong candidate for the Teacher Education Program. If there are any questions I can answer, please feel free to contact me.

Mrinal Mukherjee

Mrinal Mukherjee
Graduate Student Instructor

C. For an average student

30 June 2007

I am pleased to write a letter of recommendation for George Gump as part of his application to dentistry school. As George's instructor for Math 235 (Set Theory), I found him to be a conscientious and hardworking student. The course was not required for George's major; he took it out of intellectual interest, and he approached the material with the same curiosity and determination that he applies in biology and medicine.

George's work on the problem sets and exams demonstrated careful attention to detail. He was also able and willing to articulate his questions about the more abstract notions of set theory, a genuine asset for many of his classmates and the class dynamic as a whole.

George is an extremely personable young man who seems equally comfortable with his peers and with faculty. He has talked with me about his goal of becoming a dentist, and I have enjoyed seeing such enthusiasm in an undergraduate about a professional career. George's commitment to the field and his hard work in pursuing his goals will serve him well in dentistry school.

Please contact me if I can answer any further questions.

Sincerely,

Kelly Atkins, Ph.D.

Kelly Atkins, Ph.D.
Lecturer

Appendix H
Midterm Feedback Form

Midterm Feedback Form

You can use a selection from the questions below for a midterm feedback form.

1. In what ways would you adjust the reading assignments for the second half of the term?

2. How could our discussions of the readings be made more helpful and relevant to your own work?

3. For the next two long papers, how much freedom in the choice of topic would you like, compared to earlier assignments?

4. How could I make my comments on your papers more helpful for you?

5. What changes would you like to see in our in-class discussions?

6. Have you found keeping a journal to be a useful activity? How often do you think you should write entries, and how often should I read them?

7. What suggestions do you have for making peer writing workshops more effective?

8. Please complete the following.

   I would like to see more time devoted to:

   I would like to see less time devoted to:

   I am still confused about:

9. Please comment on any other aspects of the course that are on your mind.

Index

Annotated text, with questions, 190–91
Arguments, problematic, 119
Arrival to class, timing of, 24–25
Assigning student responsibility, 175–77
Attendance: non-attendance, 79; policy, 23, 28; problems, 111–12; taking of, 25–26
Authority, when teaching, 6, 15, 22

Background, providing personal, 15–19
Balance, between teaching and school, 175–81

Cheating, 131–32
Class: addressing problems in, 43–44; before first session of, 11–13; dynamics of, 52, 159–60; establishing policies for, 22; first session of, 24–29; preparation for, 31–44, 178; starting time of, 12; time management during, 38–39
Class participation, 24. See also Grading, and class participation
Class plans: consolidating lists, 91–92; debates, 85–89; development of, 12; exam preparation, 96–99; grammar and usage reviews, 99–101; guest speakers, 93–95; information exchange, 83–85; paper workshops, 101–5; pros and cons, 89–90; video presentations, 92–93. See also Lesson plans
Classroom: arrangement of, 39–40, 46; location of, 11–12
Close reading, 48–49
Closure. See Discussion, wrapping up of; Wrapping up
Clothes, for teaching, 13–14
Coffee shops, meeting in, 107
Collaboration: among students, 69–71; among teachers, 1
Consolidating lists, 91–92
Copying, 13

Counseling services: academic, 114; mental health related, 114
Crushes, 121–22
Culture, issues of, 17–18, 56

Deadlines, 23
Debates, 85–89
Devil's advocate, acting as, 57
Directors of undergraduate studies, 111, 119, 124–25, 129–31, 137
Discussion: facilitating of, 39–40, 53–55; questions for, 49–51; vs. task-based participation, 45–46; wrapping up of, 62–64
Discussion classes, 37, 45–64; sample lesson plan for, 187–88
Drop/add policy, 13, 26

E-mail, 20, 109–11; "cc"-ing of, 111, 124; and class e-mail group, 21; keeping records of, 111; tone of, 110
Evaluation, by students: final, 171–72; midterm, 170–71; sample of midterm, 200
Exams: in-class reviews for, 160–62; missed, 23, 162–63; preparation for, 96–99; proctoring of, 131. See also Grading, of exams
Experimental laboratories. See Laboratories
Experiments, failed, 79

Facilitating. See Discussion, facilitating
Feedback: to professor, 41; from professor, 41–42; from students, 73–74, 166–74. See also Professor, relationship with; Evaluation, by students
Final grades. See Grading, and calculating final grade
First day of the term, 11–30
Freewriting, 47, 73–74

Gender, issues of, 16–17, 56
Goals, for teaching. *See* Teaching goals
Grade books, 141–43
Grade complaints, 132–38
Graded material, returning of, 158–60, 164–65
Grades, posting of, 165
Grading, 141–65; and calculating final grade, 163–65; and class participation, 163–64; of exams, 132, 143–45; of final exams and papers, 164; and group work, 156–58; of lab reports, 155–56; and late work, 162; and missed exams, 162–63; of papers, 145–54; of paper workshops, 103–4; of problem sets, 74, 154–55; setting policy for, 23, 28
Grading curve, 152–53
Grammar and usage reviews, 99–101
Grouping strategies, 86
Guest speakers, 93–95
Guidelines: for in-class collaboration on problem sets, 71; for paper workshops, 192–94; for peer response, 195–96; for student presentations of problem sets, 72–73; for teaching assistant–led problem set review, 69

Homework, late, 23. *See also* Grading, and late work

Icebreakers, 26–28
Information cards, 24, 26
Information exchange, 83–85
Internet, appropriate use of, 125–26
Introduction, of self, 15–19, 24–25, 28

Laboratories, 75–82; common problems with, 79–80; equipment in, 76; and groups, 76–77; safety rules for, 76; weekly preparation for, 75
Lab reports, 80–82; expectations for, 81; and groups, 81–82; purpose of, 80–81; teaching from, 81, 82
Language: and accents, 19; and problematic terminology, 2–3, 118
Late work. *See* Grading, and late work; Homework, late
Learning disabilities, 23, 112–14
Lecture classes, 37–38, 39–40, 67; sample lesson plan for, 189
Lesson format, 36–38; for discussion

classes, 37; for lecture classes, 37–38; and structured student activities, 38
Lesson plans, 33–39; and allotting time, 35; and bureaucratic details, 36; format of, 36–38; for problem sets, 66–67; samples of, 187–89
Letters of recommendation, 138–40; samples of, 197–99
List, making of, for discussion, 46–47

Marks, cryptic, 149
Math anxiety, 66
Meta-teaching, 53, 168–69
Missed exams. *See* Grading, and missed exams

Names: of students, 11, 24, 26; of teaching assistant, 15
Non-attendance. *See* Attendance, non-attendance
Notes, facilitating student, 34

Office hours, 21, 106–9
Organization, of classroom. *See* Classroom, arrangement of
Organization, personal, 13

Pair and share, 47–48, 58
Papers: assignment of, 146; revision of, 153–54. *See also* Grading, of papers
Paper workshops, 101–5; and final editing exercise, 104–5; guidelines for, 192–94
Peer pressure, 51
Peer response, guidelines for writing, 195–96
Perspective, maintaining, 9
Phone numbers, 20–21
Plagiarism, 22, 23, 28, 125–31
Preparation, advance, by students, 33
Problem sets, 65–74; function of, 65; grading of, 74; review of, 67–69; setting ground rules for, 66; and student collaboration, 69–71; and student presentations, 71–73
Professor: and "cc"-ing e-mail, 111; and dealing with cheating, 132; and dealing with plagiarism, 127, 129–31; and dealing with problem students, 119, 125, 137; relationship with, 41–43, 75
Pronoun use, of generic *they*, 2–3

Proofreading, guide sheet for, 105
Pros and cons, 89–90

Race, issues of, 17–18, 56
Revision, of student work. *See* Papers, revision of

Safe space, 56
Sample precinct, 73
Scheduling, of teaching activities, 177–80
Self-preservation, 180–81
Sensitive material, 56–57
Sexual harassment, 122–25
Sexual orientation, 16, 56
Small group activities, 48
Social activities, with students, 120–21
Staff, administrative, 12
Structured student activities, 38
Student conferences, 169–70
Student participation, initiating of, 46–49
Student presentations, 71–73
Student readings, 49
Students: establishing contact with, 20–22; expecting advance preparation from, 33; fraternizing with, 120–22; one-on-one interaction with, 106–40; placing in groups, 76–77, 86; withdrawal of, 112, 117
Students, types of: antagonistic, 60, 117–19; with attendance problems, 111–12; bomb-dropper, 61; discussion-hog, 60; discussion-stopping, 57–62; dis-
ruptive, 58–62; inattentive, 80; with learning disabilities, 112–14; newspaper reader, 59; non-participating, 51–53, 58, 79; with persistent complaints, 137–38; with personal problems, 114–17; quiet, 53, 58; silent glarer, 61–62; whisperer, 59–60
Syllabus, 22–24; reviewing of, 28; sample of, 185–86

Teaching: agonies of, 7–8; joys of, 6–7
Teaching assistant, as terminology, 2
Teaching bag, 13, 15
Teaching goals, 31–32; prioritizing of, 32–33
Teaching persona, 5–6
Texts, required, 23
Time, management of, 28–29, 35, 38–39, 178–80

Unfair exam questions, 145

Video presentations, 92–93

Wrapping up: and consolidating lists, 92; and debates, 88–89; and exam preparation, 98–99; and grammar and usage reviews, 100–101; and guest speakers, 95; and information exchange, 84–85; and lab sessions, 79; and paper workshops, 103; and pros and cons, 90; and video presentations, 93
Withdrawal. *See* Students, withdrawal of